LITU[
TIME BOMBS
IN VATICAN II

The Destruction of Catholic Faith
Through Changes in Catholic Worship

MW01281757

To Lisa,
With Love.
from,
mom & John

Archbishop Annibale Bugnini, chief architect of
the New Rite of Mass which was
composed after Vatican Council II (1962-1965) and
imposed upon the Church in 1969.

In 1975 Pope Paul VI took action to remove Archbishop Bugnini
from his powerful position as Secretary of the Congregation for
Divine Worship: the Holy Father dissolved the Congregation and
assigned the Archbishop to Iran. (See p. 16.) Evidence shows that
the Pope did this because he believed Archbishop Bugnini to be a
Freemason. (See pp. 16-18.) Archbishop Bugnini died in Teheran
in 1982.

Archbishop Bugnini described the liturgical reform as "a major
conquest of the Catholic Church." (See pp. 58-59.) The New Rite of
Mass (*Novus Ordo Missae*) which was the centerpiece of that
reform continues to be celebrated in almost every Catholic church
(of the Roman Rite) in the entire world.

LITURGICAL
TIME BOMBS
IN VATICAN II

The Destruction of Catholic Faith
Through Changes in Catholic Worship

Michael Davies

TAN BOOKS AND PUBLISHERS, INC.
Rockford, Illinois 61105

Copyright © 2003 by TAN Books and Publishers, Inc. This book is expanded from sections of the author's earlier works entitled *Pope John's Council* and *Pope Paul's New Mass*—Volumes II and III of his trilogy entitled *Liturgical Revolution*.

ISBN 0-89555-773-8

Cover illustration: Nuns holding urns of incense at the altar during the consecration of the new Cathedral of Our Lady of the Angels in Los Angeles, California by Cardinal Mahoney on September 2, 2002. *Los Angeles Times* photo by Beatrice De Gea. Photo used by arrangement with Tribune Media Services International.

The cover photo illustrates the disintegration of the Catholic liturgy which has taken place as a result of the liturgical reforms—both unauthorized and authorized—that were inaugurated as the result of the Second Vatican Council (held from 1962-1965). Shown here is a clear violation of the immemorial Catholic traditions of liturgical rites being performed by a male clergy and male acolytes, in an enclosed sanctuary before an altar of traditional specifications, facing east, according to ancient Latin rituals—which do not include dancing or other invented ceremonies.

Printed and bound in the United States of America.

TAN BOOKS AND PUBLISHERS, INC.
P.O. Box 424
Rockford, Illinois 61105

2003

This book is dedicated to the memory of
Walter L. Matt,
1915-2002,
who, more than any other individual,
during the disastrous decades for the Church
which followed the Second Vatican Council,
inspired and led Catholics in the United States,
through the pages of *The Remnant*,
to remain faithful to the traditions received
from the Fathers of old, and above all,
to the Traditional Latin Mass,
spoken of by Fr. Frederick Faber as
"the most beautiful thing this side of Heaven."

"I am convinced that the crisis in the Church that we are experiencing is to a large extent due to the disintegration of the liturgy."   — *Joseph Cardinal Ratzinger*
                                        (See page 37).

"Subsequent changes were more radical than those intended by Pope John and the bishops who passed the decree on the liturgy. His sermon at the end of the first session shows that Pope John did not suspect what was being planned by the liturgical experts."
                                        — *John Cardinal Heenan*
                                        (See page 25).

"These 'time bombs' were ambiguous passages inserted in the official documents by the liberal *periti* or experts—passages which would be interpreted in an untraditional, progressivist sense after the Council closed."
                                        — *Michael Davies*
                                        (See page 23).

"It would be false to identify this liturgical renewal with the reform of rites decided on by Vatican II. This reform goes back much further and goes forward far beyond the conciliar prescriptions. The liturgy is a permanent workshop."   — *Father Joseph Gelineau*
                                        (See page 46).

"One statement we can make with certainty is that the new *Ordo* of the Mass that has now emerged would not have been endorsed by the majority of the Council Fathers."
                                        — *Msgr. Klaus Gamber*
                                        (See page 19).

"The traditional Roman rite, more than one thousand years old, has been destroyed."   — *Msgr. Klaus Gamber*
                                        (See page 69).

CONTENTS

LITURGICAL
TIME BOMBS
IN VATICAN II

The Destruction of Catholic Faith
Through Changes in Catholic Worship

"Ridiculum est, et satis abominabile dedecus, ut traditiones, quas antiquitus a patribus suscepimus, infringi patiamur."

"It is absurd, and a detestable shame, that we should suffer those traditions to be changed which we have received from the fathers of old."

—*The Decretals* (Dist. xii, 5)
Cited by St. Thomas Aquinas in the
Summa Theologica, II, I, Q. 97, art. 2.

LITURGICAL TIME BOMBS IN VATICAN II

Plans for a Liturgical Revolution?

During the first session of the Second Vatican Council, in the debate on the Constitution on the Sacred Liturgy, Cardinal Alfredo Ottaviani asked: "Are these Fathers planning a revolution?" The Cardinal was old and partly blind. He spoke from the heart about a subject that moved him deeply:

> Are we seeking to stir up wonder, or perhaps scandal among the Christian people, by introducing changes in so venerable a rite, that has been approved for so many centuries and is now so familiar? The rite of Holy Mass should not be treated as if it were a piece of cloth to be refashioned according to the whim of each generation.[1]

So concerned was the elderly Cardinal at the revolutionary potential of the Constitution, and having no prepared text, due to his very poor sight, he exceeded the ten-minute time limit for speeches. At a signal from Cardinal Alfrink, who was presiding at the session, a technician switched off the microphone, and Cardinal Ottaviani stumbled back to his seat in humiliation. The Council Fathers clapped with glee, and the journalists to whose dictatorship Father Louis Bouyer claimed that the Council had surrendered itself were even more gleeful when they wrote their reports that night, and when they wrote their books at the end of the

---

1. Michael Davies, *Pope John's Council* (Dickinson, TX: Angelus Press, 1977), p. 93. www.angeluspress.org

session.[2] While we laugh, we do not think, and had they not been laughing, at least some of the bishops may have wondered whether perhaps Cardinal Ottaviani might have had a point. He did indeed.

A liturgical revolution had been planned, and the Council's Constitution on the Sacred Liturgy, *Sacrosanctum Concilium* (CSL), was the instrument by which it was to be achieved. Very few of the 3,000 bishops present in St. Peter's would have endorsed the document had they suspected its true nature, but it would have been surprising had they done so. In his book, *La Nouvelle Messe*, Professor Louis Salleron remarks that far from seeing it as a means of initiating a revolution, the ordinary layman would have considered the CSL as the crowning achievement of the work of liturgical renewal that had been in progress for a hundred years.[3]

The Liturgical Movement

Let there be no mistake, there was great need and great scope for liturgical renewal within the Roman rite, but a renewal within the correct sense of the term, using the existing liturgy to its fullest potential. This was the aim of the liturgical movement initiated by Dom Prosper Guéranger and endorsed by Pope St. Pius X. It was defined by Dom Oliver Rousseau, O.S.B., as "the renewal of fervour for the liturgy among the clergy and the faithful." In his study of the Liturgical Movement, Father Didier Bonneterre writes:

---

2. "I do not know whether, as we are told, the Council has freed us from the tyranny of the Roman Curia, but what is sure is that, willy-nilly, it has handed us over (after having first surrendered itself) to the dictatorship of the journalists and particularly the most incompetent and irresponsible among them."—L. Bouyer, *The Decomposition of Catholicism* (Chicago: Franciscan Herald Press, 1970), p. 3.
3. Louis Salleron, *La Nouvelle Messe* (Paris: Nouvelles Éditions Latines, 1976), p. 17.

In 1903 the person who was to give the movement a defi-
nite impetus had just ascended to the See of Peter—St. Pius
X. Gifted with an immense pastoral experience, this saintly
pope suffered terribly from the decadence of liturgical life.
But he knew that a trend for renewal was developing, and he
decided to do his utmost to ensure that it bring forth good
fruits. That is why on November 22, 1903, he published his
famous *motu proprio "Tra le Sollecitudini,"* restoring Gregorian chant. In this document he inserted the vital sentence
which went on to play a determining role in the evolution of
the Liturgical Movement: "Our keen desire being that the
true Christian spirit may once more flourish, cost what it
may, and be maintained among all the faithful, We deem it
necessary to provide before anything else for the sanctity
and dignity of the temple, in which the faithful assemble for
... [the purpose] of acquiring this spirit from its primary and
indispensable source, which is the active participation in the
most holy mysteries and the public and solemn prayer of the
Church." (*Tra le Sollecitudini*, November 22, 1903).[4]

For St. Pius X, as for Dom Guéranger, writes Father
Bonneterre, "the liturgy is essentially theocentric; it is for
the worship of God rather than for the teaching of the faithful. Nevertheless, this great pastor underlined an important
aspect of the liturgy: it is educative of the true Christian
spirit. But let us stress that this function of the liturgy is
only secondary."[5] The tragedy of the Liturgical Movement
was that it would make this secondary aspect of the liturgy
the primary aspect, as is made manifest today in any typical parish celebration of the New Mass. Father Bonneterre
has nothing but praise for the initial stages of the movement: "Born of Dom Guéranger's genius and the
indomitable energy of St. Pius X, the movement at this time
brought magnificent fruits of spiritual renewal."[6]

The Modernist heresy at the beginning of the twentieth

---

4. Rev. Fr. Didier Bonneterre, *The Liturgical Movement: Guéranger to
   Beauduin to Bugnini* (Kansas City, MO: Angelus Press, 2002), p. 9.
5. Bonneterre, p. 10.
6. Bonneterre, p. 17.

century was driven underground by St. Pius X.[7] Father
Bonneterre claims that Modernist theologians who could no
longer propagate their theories in public saw in the Liturgical Movement the ideal Trojan Horse for their revolution
and that, from the 1920's onward, it became clear that the
Liturgical Movement had been diverted from its original
admirable aims. He writes:

> It was easy for all the revolutionaries to hide themselves
> in the belly of such a large carcass. Before *Mediator Dei*
> [Pius XII, 1947], who among the Catholic hierarchy was con-
> cerned about liturgy? What vigilance was applied to detect-
> ing this particularly subtle form of practical Modernism?[8]

The early leaders of the movement were, writes Father
Bonneterre, "largely overtaken by the generation of the new
liturgists of the various preconciliar liturgical commissions." He describes this new generation as the "young
wolves." In any revolution it is almost routine for the first
moderate revolutionaries to be replaced or even eradicated
by more radical revolutionaries, as was the case with the
Russian Revolution when the Mensheviks (majority) were
ousted by the Bolsheviks (minority). Just as nothing could
prevent the rise to power of the Bolsheviks, nothing could
prevent the triumph of the young wolves:

> After the Second World War the movement became a force
> that nothing could stop. Protected from on high by eminent
> prelates, the new liturgists took control little by little of the
> Commission for Reform of the Liturgy founded by Pius XII,
> and influenced the reforms devised by this Commission at
> the end of the pontificate of Pius XII and at the beginning of
> that of John XXIII. Already masters, thanks to the Pope, of
> the preconciliar liturgical commission, the new liturgists got
> the Fathers of the Council to accept a self-contradictory and

---

7. The story of the Modernist heresy is told in my book *Partisans of Error*
(Long Prairie, Minnesota: Neumann Press, 1983). www.neumannpress.com
8. Bonneterre, p. 93.

ambiguous document, the constitution *Sacrosanctum Concilium*. Pope Paul VI, Cardinal Lercaro and Fr. Bugnini, themselves very active members of the Italian Liturgical Movement, directed the efforts of the *Consilium* which culminated in the promulgation of the New Mass.[9]

The most influential of the young wolves, the great architect of the Vatican II liturgical revolution, was Father Annibale Bugnini. Father Bonneterre recounts a visit by this Italian liturgist to a liturgical convention which was held at Thieulin near Chartres in the late 1940's, at which forty religious superiors and seminary rectors were present, making clear the extent of the influence of the liturgical Bolsheviks on the Church establishment in France. He cites a Father Duployé as stating:

> Some days before the reunion at Thieulin, I had a visit from an Italian Lazarist, Fr. Bugnini, who had asked me to obtain an invitation for him. The Father listened very attentively, without saying a word, for four days. During our return journey to Paris, as the train was passing along the Swiss Lake at Versailles, he said to me: "I admire what you are doing, but the greatest service I can render you is never to say a word in Rome about all that I have just heard."[10]

Father Bonneterre comments: "This revealing text shows us one of the first appearances of the 'gravedigger of the Mass,' a revolutionary more clever than the others, he who killed the Catholic liturgy before disappearing from the official scene."[11]

The Rise and Fall and Rise and Fall of Annibale Bugnini

Before discussing the time bombs in the Council texts,

---

9. Bonneterre, p. 94.
10. Bonneterre, p. 52.
11. *Ibid.*

more specifically those in its Constitution on the Sacred Liturgy, which would lead to the destruction of the Roman Rite, it is necessary to examine the role of Annibale Bugnini, the individual most responsible for placing them there and detonating them after the Constitution had won the approval of the Council Fathers.

Annibale Bugnini was born in Civitella de Lego (Italy) in 1912. He began his theological studies in the Congregation of the Mission (the Vincentians) in 1928 and was ordained in this Order in 1936. For ten years he did parish work in a Roman suburb, and then, from 1947 to 1957, was involved in writing and editing the missionary publications of his Order. In 1947, he also began his active involvement in the field of specialized liturgical studies when he began a twenty-year period as the director of *Ephemerides liturgicae*, one of Italy's best-known liturgical publications. He contributed to numerous scholarly publications, wrote articles on the liturgy for various encyclopaedias and dictionaries, and had a number of books published on both the scholarly and popular level.

Father Bugnini was appointed Secretary to Pope Pius XII's Commission for Liturgical Reform in 1948. In 1949 he was made a Professor of Liturgy in the Pontifical *Propaganda Fide* (Propagation of the Faith) University; in 1955 he received a similar appointment in the Pontifical Institute of Sacred Music; he was appointed a Consultor to the Sacred Congregation of Rites in 1956; and in 1957 he was appointed Professor of Sacred Liturgy in the Lateran University. In 1960, Father Bugnini was placed in a position which enabled him to exert an important, if not decisive, influence upon the history of the Church: he was appointed Secretary to the Preparatory Commission on the Liturgy for the Second Vatican Council.[12] He was the moving spirit behind the drafting of the preparatory *schema* (plural *schemata*), the draft document which was to be placed

---

12. Biographical details of Archbishop Bugnini are provided in *Notitiae*, No. 70, February 1972, pp. 33-34.

before the Council Fathers for discussion. Carlo Falconi, an "ex-priest" who has left the Church but keeps in close contact with his friends in the Vatican, refers to the preparatory *schema* as "the Bugnini draft."[13] It is of the greatest possible importance to bear in mind the fact that, as was stressed in 1972 in Father Bugnini's own journal, *Notitiae* (official journal of the Sacred Congregation for Divine Worship), the Liturgy Constitution that the Council Fathers eventually passed was substantially identical to the draft *schema* which he had steered through the Preparatory Commission.[14]

According to Father P. M. Gy, O.P., a French liturgist who was a consultor to the pre-conciliar Commission on the Liturgy, Father Bugnini "was a happy choice as secretary":

> He had been secretary of the commission for reform set up by Pius XII. He was a gifted organizer and possessed an open-minded, pastoral spirit. Many people noted how, with Cardinal Cicognani, he was able to imbue the discussion with the liberty of spirit recommended by Pope John XXIII.[15]

The Bugnini *schema* was accepted by a plenary session of the Liturgical Preparatory Commission in a vote taken on January 13, 1962. But the President of the Commission, the eighty-year old Cardinal Gaetano Cicognani, had the foresight to realize the dangers implicit in certain passages. Father Gy writes: "The program of reform was so vast that it caused the president, Cardinal Gaetano Cicognani, to hesitate."[16] Unless the Cardinal could be persuaded to sign the *schema,* it would be blocked. It could not go through without his signature, even though it had been approved by a majority of the Commission. Father Bugnini needed to

---

13. Carlo Falconi, *Pope John and His Council* (London: Weidenfeld & Nicholson, 1964), p. 244.

14. *Notitiae*, No. 70, February 1972, pp. 33-34.

15. A. Flannery, *Vatican II: The Liturgy Constitution* (Dublin: Sceptre Books, 1964), p. 20.

16. Flannery, p. 23.

act. He arranged for immediate approaches to be made to Pope John, who agreed to intervene. He called for Cardinal Amleto Cicognani, his Secretary of State and the younger brother of the President of the Preparatory Commission, and told him to visit his brother and not return until the *schema* had been signed. The Cardinal complied:

> Later a *peritus* of the Liturgical Preparatory Commission stated that the old Cardinal was almost in tears as he waved the document in the air and said: "They want me to sign this but I don't know if I want to." Then he laid the document on his desk, picked up a pen, and signed it. Four days later he died.[17]

The First Fall

The Bugnini *schema* had been saved—and only just in time. Then, with the approval of Pope John XXIII, Father Bugnini was dismissed from his chair at the Lateran University and from the secretaryship of the Conciliar Liturgical Commission which was to oversee the *schema* during the conciliar debates. The reasons which prompted Pope John to take this step have not been divulged, but they must have been of a most serious nature to cause this tolerant Pontiff to act in so public and drastic a manner against a priest who had held such an influential position in the preparation for the Council. In his book *The Reform of the Liturgy*, which to a large extent is an apologia for himself and a denunciation of his critics, Bugnini blames Cardinal Arcadio Larraona for his downfall. He writes of himself in the third person:

> Of all the secretaries of the preparatory commissions, Father Bugnini was the only one not appointed secretary to the corresponding conciliar commission . . . This was Father Bugnini's first exile. At the same time that Father Bugnini

---

17. Fr. Ralph M. Wiltgen, S.V.D., *The Rhine Flows into the Tiber: A History of Vatican II* (1967; rpt. Rockford, IL: TAN, 1985), p. 141.

was dismissed from the secretariat of the conciliar commission, he was also discharged from his post as teacher of liturgy in the Pontifical Pastoral Institute of the Lateran University, and an attempt was made to take from him the chair of liturgy at the Pontifical Urban University. This repressive activity emanated directly from Cardinal Larraona and was very kindly seconded by some fellow workers who wanted better to serve the Church and the liturgy. The basis for the dismissals was the charge of being a "progressivist," "pushy," and an "iconoclast" (innuendos whispered half-aloud), accusations then echoed in turn by the Congregation of Rites, the Congregation of Seminaries, and the Holy Office. But no proof was offered, no clear justification for such serious measures.[18]

Bugnini's claim that "no proof was offered" is simply a gratuitous assertion on his part. The fact that he saw no proof in no way proves that it did not exist. Falconi condemns the dismissal of Father Bugnini as a retrograde step, but adds:

> All the same, Bugnini managed to get his draft through as far as the Council, and now it will be interesting to see if it is passed, and even more so if the draft schema of the proscribed Secretary of the Liturgical Commission should open the way for the success of other drafts of a progressive character.[19]

The dismissal of Father Bugnini was very much a case of locking the stable door after the horse had bolted. It would have helped Father Bugnini's cause had he been appointed Secretary to the Conciliar Commission (the post was given to Father Ferdinand Antonelli, O.F.M.), as he could then have guided his *schema* through the Council—but this was not essential. It was the *schema* that mattered.

Seventy-five preparatory *schemata* had been prepared for

---

18. Annibale Bugnini, *The Reform of the Liturgy 1948-1975* (Collegeville, Minnesota: The Liturgical Press, 1990), p. 30.

19. Falconi, p. 224.

the Council Fathers, the fruits of the most painstaking and meticulous preparation for a Council in the history of the Church.[20] The number was eventually reduced to twenty, and seven were selected for discussion at the first session of the Council.[21] The Bugnini *schema* was the fifth of these, and it was presumed by most bishops that the *schemata* would be debated in their numerical sequence.[22] But the other *schemata* were so orthodox that the liberals could not accept them—even as a basis for discussion. At the instigation of Father Edward Schillebeeckx, O.P., a Belgian-born Professor of Dogmatics at the Catholic University of Nijmegen, the *schemata* were rejected with one exception—the Bugnini *schema*. This, he said, was "an admirable piece of work."[23] It was announced at the second general congregation of the Council on October 16, 1962, that the sacred liturgy was the first item on the agenda for examination by the Fathers.[24] *Notitiae* looked back on this with considerable satisfaction in 1972, remarking that the Bugnini preparatory *schema* was the only one that was eventually passed without substantial alteration.[25] Father Wiltgen comments:

> It should be noted that the liturgical movement had been active in Europe for several decades, and that quite a large number of bishops and *periti* from the Rhine countries had been appointed by Pope John to the preparatory commission on the liturgy. As a result, they had succeeded in inserting their ideas into the *schema* and gaining approval for what they considered a very acceptable document.[26]

As for the other *schemata*, one prominent Council Father, Archbishop Marcel Lefebvre, wrote:

---

20. Wiltgen, p. 22.
21. *Ibid.*
22. *Ibid.*
23. *Ibid.*, p. 23.
24. Bugnini, p. 29.
25. *Notitiae*, No. 70, p. 34.
26. Wiltgen, p. 23.

Now you know what happened at the Council. A fortnight after its opening not one of the prepared *schemata* remained, not one! All had been turned down, all had been condemned to the wastepaper basket. Nothing remained, not a single sentence. All had been thrown out.[27]

Bugnini's allies who had worked with him on preparing the *schema* now had the task of securing its acceptance by the bishops without any substantial alterations. They did so with a degree of success that certainly exceeded the hopes of their wildest dreams. They seem to have presumed that the bishops would be a bunch of "useful idiots," men who preferred to laugh rather than to think. "It was all good fun," wrote Archbishop R. J. Dwyer, one of the most erudite of the American bishops. "And when the vote came round, like wise Sir Joseph Porter, K.C.M., 'We always voted at our party's call; we never thought of thinking for ourselves at all.' That way you can save yourself a whole world of trouble."[28] The Bugnini *schema* received the almost unanimous approval of the Council Fathers on December 7, 1962 and became Vatican II's "Constitution on the Sacred Liturgy" (CSL). But the Constitution contained no more than general guidelines; therefore, to achieve total victory, Father Bugnini and his cohorts needed to obtain the power to interpret and implement it.

27. Marcel Lefebvre, *A Bishop Speaks* (Kansas City, MO: Angelus Press, 1987), p. 131.
28. *Twin Circle*, October 26, 1963, p. 2.

The Second Rise

The Rhine Group[29] pressed for the establishment of postconciliar commissions with the authority to interpret the CSL. It "feared that the progressive measures adopted by the Council might be blocked by conservative forces near the Pope once the Council Fathers had returned home."[30] Cardinal Heenan, of Westminster, England, had warned of the danger if the Council *periti* were given the power to interpret the Council to the world. "God forbid that this should happen!" he told the others.[31] This was just what did happen. The members of these commissions were "chosen with the Pope's approval, for the most part, from the ranks of the Council *periti*. The task of the commissions is to put into effect the Council decrees . . . and, when necessary, to interpret the Council institutions, decrees, and declarations."[32] On March 5, 1964, *l'Osservatore Romano* announced the establishment of the Commission for the Implementation of the Constitution on the Liturgy, which became known as the *Consilium*. The initial membership consisted mainly of members of the Commission that had drafted the Constitution. Father Bugnini was appointed to the position of Secretary of the *Consilium* on February 29, 1964. What prompted Pope Paul VI to appoint Bugnini to this crucially important position after he had been pre-

---

29. In the Preface to *The Rhine Flows into the Tiber* (p. 1), Father Wiltgen explains that the "predominant influence" during the Second Vatican Council came from Council Fathers and *periti* (experts) from the "countries along the Rhine river—Germany, Austria, Switzerland, France, the Netherlands—and from nearby Belgium. Because this group exerted a predominant influence over the Second Vatican Council, I have titled my book *The Rhine Flows into the Tiber.*" This is certainly the most informative book written on what really happened at Vatican II, and it should be owned by every Catholic taking a serious interest in events since the Council. The six countries named were those in which the Liturgical Movement had been most active and in which liberal ideas were most manifest.

30. Wiltgen, pp. 287-288.

31. *Ibid.*, p. 210.

32. *The Tablet* (London), January 22, 1966, p. 114.

vented by Pope John XXIII from becoming Secretary of the Conciliar Commission is probably something that we shall never know.

In theory, the *Consilium* was an advisory body, and the reforms it devised had to be implemented by either the Sacred Congregation for Rites or the Sacred Congregation for the Discipline of the Sacraments. These congregations had been established as part of Pope Paul's reform of the Roman Curia, promulgated on August 15, 1967. Father Bugnini's influence as Secretary of the *Consilium* was increased when he was appointed Under-Secretary to the Sacred Congregation for Rites.[33] On May 8, 1969, Pope Paul promulgated the Apostolic Constitution *Sacra Rituum Congregatio,* which ended the existence of the *Consilium* as a separate body; it was incorporated into the newly established Sacred Congregation for Divine Worship as a special commission which would retain its members and consultors and remain until the reform of the liturgy had been completed. *Notitiae,* official journal of the *Consilium,* became the journal of the new Congregation. Father Annibale Bugnini was appointed Secretary of the Sacred Congregation for Divine Worship and became more powerful than ever. It is certainly no exaggeration to claim that what in fact had happened was that the *Consilium,* in other words Father Bugnini, had taken over the Sacred Congregation for Divine Worship. The April-June 1969 issue of *Notitiae* announced Father Bugnini's appointment, stating:

> This number of *Notitiae* appears under the direction of the new Congregation for Divine Worship. Pope Paul VI, at the end of the 28 April Consistory, made the announcement and gave it an official character with the Apostolic Constitution "Sacred Congregation of Rites" of 8 May. The new Congregation will continue on a firmer juridical foundation, with more effectiveness and renewed commitment, the work accomplished by the *Consilium* in the past five years, linking itself with the Council, its preparatory commission, and the entire

---

33. *Notitiae,* No. 70, February 1972, p. 34.

liturgical movement . . . The *Consilium* continues as a particular commission of the Congregation until the completion
of the reform.

Father Bugnini was now in the most influential position
possible to consolidate and extend the revolution behind
which he had been the moving spirit and the principle of
continuity. Nominal heads of commissions, congregations,
and the *Consilium* came and went—Cardinal Lercaro, Cardinal Gut, Cardinal Tabera, Cardinal Knox—but Father
Bugnini always remained. He attributed this to the Divine
Will: "The Lord willed that from those early years a whole
series of providential circumstances should thrust me fully,
and indeed in a privileged way, *in medias res*, and that I
should remain there in charge of the secretariat."[34] His services would be rewarded by his being consecrated a bishop
and then being elevated to the rank of Titular Archbishop of
Dioclentiana, as announced on January 7, 1972.

The Imposition of the New Rite of Mass

What the experts were planning had already been made
clear on October 24, 1967 in the Sistine Chapel, when what
was described as the *Missa Normativa* was celebrated
before the Synod of Bishops by Father Annibale Bugnini
himself, its chief architect. Since he had been appointed secretary of the post-Vatican II Liturgy Commission, he had
the power to orchestrate the composition of the New Rite of
Mass which he had envisaged in the *schema* that he had
prepared before his dismissal by John XXIII—the *schema*
which had been passed virtually unchanged by the Council
Fathers. As already remarked, why Pope Paul VI appointed
to this key position a man who had been dismissed by his
predecessor is a mystery which will probably never be
answered.

Fewer than half the bishops present voted in favor of the

---

34. Bugnini, p. xxiii.

Missa Normativa, but the far-from-satisfied majority was ignored with the arrogance which was to become the most evident characteristic of the liturgical establishment, to which the Council Fathers had been naive enough to entrust the implementation of the Constitution on the Sacred Liturgy. The *Missa Normativa* would be imposed on Catholics of the Roman Rite by Pope Paul VI in 1969, with a few changes, as the *Novus Ordo Missae:* the New Order of Mass.

In 1974 Archbishop Bugnini explained that his reform had been divided into four stages—firstly, the transition from Latin to the vernacular; secondly, the reform of the liturgical books; thirdly, the translation of the liturgical books; and fourthly, the adaptation or "incarnation" of the Roman form of the liturgy into the usages and mentality of each individual Church.[35] This process (which would mean the complete elimination of any remaining vestiges of the Roman Rite) had already begun, he claimed, and would be "pursued with ever increasing care and preparation."[36]

The Second Fall

At the very moment when his power had reached its zenith, Archbishop Bugnini was in effect dismissed—this was his second fall—to the dismay of liberal Catholics throughout the world. What happened was that the Archbishop's entire Congregation was dissolved and merged with the Congregation for the Sacraments under the terms of Pope Paul's Apostolic Constitution *Constans Nobis*, published in *l' Osservatore Romano* (English edition) of July 31, 1975. The new congregation was entitled the Sacred Congregation for the Sacraments and Divine Worship. The name Bugnini did not appear in the list of appointments. Liberals throughout the world were dismayed. *The Tablet*, in England, and its extreme liberal counterpart in the

---

35. *Notitiae*, No. 92, April 1974, p. 126.
36. *Ibid.*

United States, the *National Catholic Reporter*, carried an indignant report by Desmond O'Grady:

> Archbishop Annibale Bugnini, who, as Secretary of the abolished Congregation for Divine Worship, was the key figure in the Church's liturgical reform, is not a member of the new Congregation. Nor, despite his lengthy experience was he consulted in the planning of it. He heard of its creation while on holiday at Fiuggi . . . the abrupt way in which this was done does not augur well for the Bugnini line of encouragement for reform in collaboration with local hierarchies. . . Msgr. Bugnini conceived the next ten years' work as concerned principally with the incorporation of local usages into the liturgy . . . He represented the continuity of the post-conciliar liturgical reform.[37]

L'Osservatore Romano carried the following announcement in its English edition, on January 15, 1976: "5 January: The Holy Father has appointed Apostolic Pro Nuncio in Iran His Excellency the Most Reverend Annibale Bugnini, C. M., titular Archbishop of Dioclentiana." This was clearly an artificial post created to gloss over the fact that the Archbishop had been banished.

In his book *The Devastated Vineyard*, published in 1973, Dietrich von Hildebrand rightly observed concerning Bugnini that: "Truly, if one of the devils in C. S. Lewis's *The Screwtape Letters* had been entrusted with the ruin of the liturgy, he could not have done it better."[38] This is a statement based on an objective assessment of the reform itself. It is beyond dispute that whether or not the Roman Rite has been destroyed deliberately, it has been destroyed. (See pages 69-70 herein.) If this result is simply the consequence of ill-judged decisions by well-meaning men, the objective fact remains unchanged: they could not have destroyed the Roman Rite more effectively had they done so deliberately.

---

37. *The Tablet*, August 30, 1975, p. 828.
38. Dietrich von Hildebrand, *The Devastated Vineyard* (Chicago: Franciscan Herald Press, 1973), p. 71.

But the thoroughness of the destruction caused many to wonder whether it might be more than the result of ill-considered policies. It came as no great surprise when, in April of 1976, Tito Casini, Italy's leading Catholic writer, publicly accused Archbishop Bugnini of being a Freemason.[39] On October 8, 1976, *Le Figaro* published a report stating that Archbishop Bugnini denied ever having had any Masonic affiliation.

I have made my own investigation into the affair and can vouch for the authenticity of the following facts. A Roman priest of the very highest reputation came into possession of evidence which he considered proved Archbishop Bugnini to be a Freemason. He had this information placed into the hands of Pope Paul VI with the warning that if action were not taken at once, he would be bound in conscience to make the matter public. Archbishop Bugnini was then removed by means of the dissolution of his entire Congregation. I have verified these facts directly with the priest concerned, and the full facts can be found in Chapter XXIV of my book *Pope Paul's New Mass*.

An important distinction must be made here. I have not claimed that I can prove Archbishop Bugnini to have been a Mason, but that Pope Paul VI dismissed him and exiled him to Iran because *he* had been convinced that the Archbishop was a Mason. I made this same point in a letter published in the January 1980 *Homiletic and Pastoral Review,* which prompted a violent attack upon me by Archbishop Bugnini in the May 1980 issue. He denied that any of the prelates who, since Vatican II, had been accused of Masonic affiliation "ever had anything to do with Freemasonry," and he continued:

> And for Michael Davies it would be enough. [sic] But for him and his colleagues, calumniators by profession . . . I repeat what I wrote in 1976: "I do not own anything in this

---

39. Tito Casini, *Nel Fumo di Satana* (Florence: Carro di San Giovanni, 1976), p. 150.

world more precious than the pectoral cross: if one is able to prove honestly, objectively, an iota of truth of what they affirm, I am ready to return back the pectoral cross."

But, as I have already stated, I did not accuse him of being a Mason but simply pointed out that Pope Paul VI had been convinced that this was the case, and the fact that this does not constitute calumny is proved by the fact that Bugnini conceded precisely what I had alleged in his book *The Reform of the Liturgy*. Referring to his removal from his position by Pope Paul VI and the suppression of the Congregation for Divine Worship, he wrote:

> What were the reasons that led the Pope to such a drastic decision, which no one expected and which lay so heavily on the Church? I said in the preface to this book that I myself never knew any of these reasons for sure, even though, understandably in the distress of the moment, I knocked on many doors at all levels . . . There were those who ascribed the change to the "authoritarian," "almost dictatorial" way in which the secretary of the congregation supposedly managed the agency, not allowing freedom of movement to his own co-workers and limiting the role even of the cardinal prefects.[40] But when all is said and done, all this seems to be the stuff of ordinary administrative life. There must have been something more earthshaking. Toward the end of the summer a cardinal who was usually no enthusiast for the liturgical reform told me of the existence of a "dossier" which he had seen on (or brought to?) the Pope's desk and which proved that Archbishop Bugnini was a Freemason.[41]

---

40. In a footnote commenting on these complaints made by members of the Congregation for Divine Worship, Archbishop Bugnini comments: "Human deficiencies are always possible, of course, but the accusation reflects a mentality that was periodically revived among officials of the Congregation who out of ambition or defects of character, were determined to create difficulties for the secretary." This remark is typical of his insistence throughout the book that no criticism made of him can ever be justified and that those who make these criticisms have bad motives.

41. Bugnini, p. 91.

Although one is not supposed to speak ill of the dead—*de mortuis nil nisi bonum* (literally, "of the dead, nothing except good"), in an historical study such as this, objectivity demands that it be made clear that truth was not a priority with Archbishop Bugnini. In an attempt to play down the role played by the Protestant observers in his liturgical revolution, he stated: "They never intervened in the discussions and never asked to speak."[42] As is made clear in Appendix I, this is highly misleading. There is not the least doubt that the Second Vatican Council was a cause of great satisfaction to Protestants. In their final message to the Council, read by Archbishop Felici on December 4, 1965, the Observer-delegates enlarged on this theme: "Blessed be God for all that he has given us so far through the Holy Spirit, and for all that he will give us in the future." Oscar Cullmann, the noted Swiss theologian, summed up their thoughts when he declared: "The hopes of Protestants for Vatican II have not only been fulfilled, but the Council's achievements have gone far beyond what was believed possible."[43]

An Unsuspected Blueprint for Revolution

The late Monsignor Klaus Gamber was described by Cardinal Ratzinger as "the one scholar who, among the army of pseudo-liturgists, truly represents the liturgical thinking of the center of the Church."[44] As regards the attitude the Council Fathers would have taken to the changes that have been foisted upon us in the name of Vatican II, Monsignor Gamber informs us in his book *The Reform of the Roman Liturgy* that: "One statement we can make with certainty is that the new *Ordo* of the Mass that has now emerged would not have been endorsed by the majority of the Council Fathers."[45]

---

42. *Notitiae*, July-August 1974.
43. Xavier Rynne, *The Fourth Session* (London: Herder & Herder, 1966), p. 256.
44. Msgr. Klaus Gamber, *The Reform of the Roman Liturgy* (Harrison, NY: Foundation for Catholic Reform, 1993), p. xiii (Testimonial by Msgr. Nyssen).
45. *Ibid.*, p. 61.

Why then did these bishops endorse the Constitution on the Sacred Liturgy? Professor Louis Salleron has been cited as stating that the CSL appeared to be the crowning achievement of the work of liturgical renewal which had been in progress for a hundred years. Why could this have appeared to be the case when, in fact, the CSL was a blueprint for revolution? The 1,922 bishops who cast their *placet* ("Yes") votes for the Constitution on December 7, 1962 would certainly have been reassured by stipulations it contained which gave the impression that there was no possibility of any radical liturgical reform. Article 4 of the CSL certainly gives the impression that there is no danger of any drastic change in any of the existing rites of Mass, among which the Roman Rite was clearly paramount: "This most sacred Council declares that Holy Mother Church holds all lawfully acknowledged rites to be of equal authority and dignity: that she wishes to *preserve them in the future* and to foster them in every way." (Emphasis added.) But these reassuring words are qualified by the additional directive of the Council that "where necessary the rites be carefully and thoroughly revised in the light of sound tradition, and that they be given new vigor to meet the circumstances of modern times." No explanation is given as to how it is possible both to preserve and foster these rites and, at the same time, to revise them to meet certain unspecified circumstances and unspecified needs of modern times. Nor is it explained how such a revision could be carried out in the light of sound tradition when it had been the sound and invariable tradition of the Roman Rite never to undertake any drastic revision of its rites, a tradition of well over 1,000 years' standing, which had been breached only during the Protestant Reformation, when every heretical sect devised new rites to correspond with its heretical teachings.

Article 23 of the CSL requires that, in order to maintain "sound tradition," a careful investigation is to be made before revising any part of the liturgy. "This investigation should be theological, historical and pastoral." If this were not reassuring enough, Article 23 also mandates that:

"There must be no innovations unless the good of the Church genuinely and certainly requires them, and care must be taken that any new forms should in some way grow organically from forms already existing."

It is an instructive exercise to go, step by step, through the changes which have been made in the Mass, beginning with the abolition of the *Judica me* and ending with the abolition of the Last Gospel, or even the Prayers for the Conversion of Russia, and to consider carefully why the good of the Church genuinely and certainly required that each particular change *must* be made. Has the good of the Church really been enhanced because the faithful have been forbidden to kneel at the *Incarnatus est* during the Creed? Did the good of the Church genuinely, certainly, require that the doctrinally rich Offertory prayers should be abolished? To illustrate this doctrinal richness, just one of these prayers, the *Suscipe, sancte Pater*, will be examined within the context of a commentary by Father Pius Parsch, one of the best known figures of the liturgical movement.[46]

Having recited the Offertory verse, the priest unveils the chalice, takes the paten with the host of unleavened bread upon it, and, raising it up to about the level of his eyes, offers it to God with the prayer *Suscipe, sancte Pater*: "Receive, O Holy Father, Almighty and Eternal God, this spotless host which I, Thy unworthy servant, offer unto Thee, my living and true God, for mine own countless sins, offences and negligences, and for all here present; as also for all faithful Christians, living or dead, that it may avail for my own and for their salvation unto life everlasting. Amen."

This prayer—the richest in content of any of this part of the Mass—contains a whole world of dogmatic truth. Who is it that offers the sacrifice? It is the priest as representative of Christ: "which I, Thy unworthy servant, offer." To whom? To the Father, all-holy, God Almighty, "the living and true

---

46. It is sad to note that at the same time he was writing such an orthodox and even inspiring exposition of the Mass (in the 1950's), Father Parsch was taking part in unauthorized liturgical experiments. (See Bonneterre, pp. 28-29.)

God." What does he offer? "This spotless Victim." He offers
the bread, but the expression *hostia immaculata* shows that
the thoughts of the priest in this prayer do not rest there.
This bread which he holds in his hands is as yet neither *hostia* (victim) nor, properly speaking, *immaculata*. Yet already
he has its destiny in mind. It is to become the Eucharist, the
Hostia immaculata in very truth, a consummation already
anticipated in thought. And for whom is it offered? In atone-
ment for the "innumerable sins, offences and negligences" of
the priest himself. These terms are, of course, synonymous.
The liturgy frequently uses such accumulative expressions
to deepen the impression upon our minds. It is offered too for
"all those present" (*circumstantes*—standing around the
altar of sacrifice), and beyond them, for all Christians "living
or dead." All will benefit by the sacrifice which has as its
final purpose "that it may avail for my own and for their salvation unto life everlasting." The final purpose of the Mass
is, therefore, the same as that of the Sacrifice of the Cross:
the salvation of all mankind. This prayer, so rich in doctrine,
could serve as the basis for an entire treatise on the Mass.[47]

How can it possibly be argued that the good of the Church
genuinely and certainly required the abolition of this sublime prayer? Has any Catholic anywhere in the world
become more fervent in his faith as a result of its absence?
Those in the Church obsessed by false ecumenism would
certainly have argued that this prayer, and other prayers
removed from the Mass by the sixteenth-century Protestant
heretics, must be removed from the Mass to avoid offence to
our Protestant brethren. Luther referred to "all that abomination called the offertory. And from this point almost
everything stinks of oblation. Therefore casting aside all
that savours of oblation with the entire canon, let us keep
those things which are pure and holy."[48] The entire Canon

---

47. Pius Parsch, *The Liturgy of the Mass* (St. Louis: B. Herder, 1961),
    pp. 184-5.
48. Cited in F. A. Gasquet, *Edward VI and the Book of Common Prayer* (Lon-
    don: John Hodges, 1890), p. 221. Chapter XIII of this book contains a very
    detailed examination of Luther's liturgical reforms.

was indeed cast aside by Bugnini and his *Consilium*—but it was restored, to their regret, on the insistence of Pope Paul VI.[49]

It would be most enlightening to be told the exact process by which, for example, the new Offertory prayers (based on a Jewish form of grace before meals) grew from "forms already existing." The *Consilium* presumably interpreted this phrase as meaning already existing in the liturgy of *any* religion.

There is a most bitter irony in another admonition contained in Article 23: "As far as possible, notable differences between the rites used in adjacent regions are to be carefully avoided." Today it is hard to recognize that some adjacent parishes even belong to the same religion, so great is the contrast between their respective modes of celebrating Mass.

Clauses such as Article 4 and Article 23 would certainly have reassured the bishops that there would be no radical changes in the liturgy of the Mass, but there were other clauses which did indeed open the way to radical or even revolutionary change. Archbishop Lefebvre was in no doubt as to the nature of these clauses. He stated: "There were time bombs in the Council."[50] These "time bombs" were ambiguous passages inserted in the official documents by the liberal *periti* or experts—passages which would be interpreted in an untraditional, progressivist sense after the Council closed. The answer to Cardinal Ottaviani's question as to whether the Council Fathers were planning a revolution (see page 1) is that the majority of the Fathers, the 3,000 bishops,[51] most certainly were not, but that some of the influential *periti*, the experts who accompanied the bishops to Rome, definitely had this intention.

---

49. M. Davies, *Pope Paul's New Mass* (Dickinson, TX: Angelus Press, 1980), p. 329; Bugnini, p. 152, Note 30.
50. Lefebvre, p. 135.
51. 2,860 Council Fathers attended all or part of the four sessions—a combined total of 281 days. (Wiltgen, p. 287.)

The Council of the *Periti*

It is not exaggerating in any way to claim that the liberal *periti* hijacked Pope John's Council, a fact I have documented in great detail in my book on Vatican II.[52] Douglas Woodruff, one of England's outstanding Catholic scholars, was editor of *The Tablet* during the Council. In one of his reports he remarked: "For in a sense this Council has been the Council of the *periti*, silent in the aula but so effective in the commissions and at bishops' ears."[53] This is an exceptionally perceptive comment, and it would be hard to improve on "the Council of the *periti*" as a one-phrase description of Vatican II. Bishop Lucey of Cork and Ross (Ireland) stated that the *periti* were more powerful than most bishops, even though they had no vote, "because they had the ear of a Cardinal or the head of a national group of bishops, and they were influential in the drafting of Council documents. The expert . . . is the person with power."[54]

The "time bombs" referred to by Archbishop Lefebvre were, as has been explained, the ambiguous passages inserted in the official documents by the liberal *periti* which could weaken the presentation of traditional Catholic teaching: by abandoning the traditional terminology, by omissions, or by ambiguous phraseology which could be compatible with a non-Catholic interpretation. Cardinal Heenan testifies: "A determined group could wear down opposition and produce a formula patient of both an orthodox and modernistic interpretation."[55] Archbishop Lefebvre went to the extent of describing the Council documents as "a mass of ambiguities, vagueness and sentimentality, things which now clearly admit all interpretations and have left all doors open."[56] In his book *A Crown of Thorns*, Cardinal Heenan wrote:

---

52. Davies, *Pope John's Council*, Chapter 5.
53. *The Tablet*, November 27, 1965, p. 1318.
54. *Catholic Standard* (Dublin), October 17, 1973.
55. *The Tablet*, May 18, 1968.
56. Lefebvre, pp. 109-110.

The subject most fully debated was liturgical reform. It might be more accurate to say that the bishops were *under the impression* that the liturgy had been fully discussed. In retrospect it is clear that they were given the opportunity of discussing only general principles. *Subsequent changes were more radical than those intended by Pope John and the bishops* who passed the decree on the liturgy. His sermon at the end of the first session shows that *Pope John did not suspect what was being planned by the liturgical experts.* (Emphasis added).[57]

What could be clearer than this? One of the most active and erudite Council Fathers states that the liturgical experts who drafted the CSL phrased it in such a way that they could use it after the Council in a manner not foreseen by the Pope and the Bishops. To put it plainly, the Cardinal states that there was a conspiracy.

The liturgical revolution which has emerged from the Constitution has been initiated precisely on the basis of a number of carefully formulated clauses, the significance of which eluded the Council Fathers. This was evident even to an American Protestant Observer, Robert McAfee Brown, who remarked: "The Council documents themselves often implied more in the way of change than the Council Fathers were necessarily aware of when they voted."[58] In this respect he made particular mention of the Liturgy Constitution: "The Constitution opens many doors that can later be pushed even wider, and does not bind the Church to a new liturgical rigidity."[59] Those who gained control of the *Consilium*, the Committee which implemented the CSL, used these clauses in precisely the manner they had intended to use them when, as Cardinal Heenan assures us, they had inserted them into the CSL as members of the Pre-Conciliar and Conciliar Liturgical Commissions.

57. John Heenan, *A Crown of Thorns* (London: Hodder & Stoughton, 1974), p. 367.
58. R. McAfee Brown, *The Ecumenical Revolution* (New York: Doubleday, 1969), p. 210.
59. R. McAfee Brown, *Observer in Rome* (London: Methuen, 1964), p. 226.

The Constitution itself became a dead letter almost from the moment it was passed with such euphoria by the Council Fathers. It could have been used to initiate a true renewal, faithful to the authentic liturgical principles endorsed by the Popes and expounded in documents ranging from *Tra le solicitudini* of St. Pius X (1903) to the *De musica sacra et sacra liturgia* of Pope Pius XII (1958). Even Archbishop Lefebvre wrote in 1963: "Let us then admit without hesitation that some liturgical reforms were necessary . . ."[60] But discussing what might have been is the most fruitless of occupations; it is what actually happened that matters. The full extent of episcopal subservience to the diktat of the "experts" was made clear by Archbishop Lefebvre in a lecture he gave in Vienna in September of 1975. He explained that the French episcopal conference "held meetings during which they were given the exact texts of the speeches they had to make. 'You, Bishop So-and-so, you will speak on such a subject, a certain theologian will write the text for you, and all you have to do is read it.' "[61] This was not only the case with the French hierarchy. I have documented in my book *The Second Vatican Council and Religious Liberty* the extent to which bishops from the United States and other hierarchies dutifully read speeches written for them by Father John Courtney Murray in praise of the draft declaration of which he was the principal author.[62] As one American prelate expressed it: "The voices are the voices of the United States' Bishops, but the thoughts are the thoughts of John Courtney Murray."[63] The most celebrated speech during the debate on religious liberty, the most hotly contested debate of the Council, was made by Belgian Bishop Emile de Smedt on November 19, 1963. Bishop de Smedt received thunderous applause, the

---

60. Lefebvre, p. 9.
61. Marcel Lefebvre, *Pour L'Honneur de l'Eglise* (Paris: Editions de la Nouvelle Aurore, 1975), pp. 5-6.
62. M. Davies, *The Second Vatican Council and Religious Liberty* (Long Prairie, MN: Neumann Press, 1992), pp. 120-125.
63. *Ibid.*, p. 161.

greatest single outburst of the Council. The speech had, in fact, been written for him by Father Murray.[64]

According to Robert Kaiser, who reported on the Council for *Time* magazine, the battle over the CSL was won by the liberals on December 7, 1962 when the preface and first chapter were approved with only eleven dissenting votes.

> To the Council's progressives, euphoric over other battles fought and won, this was a sweet message. True, they would have to vote on other chapters, but they would be mere formalities. "Within the preface and first chapter," a member of the Liturgical Commission told me, "are the seeds of all the other reforms." It was true also that the Pope would have to ratify the action. But no one thought he would attempt to veto what the Council had spent so long achieving.[65]

He did not!

Detonating the Time Bombs

One of the first points made in the preface to the CSL is that the Council intends to "nurture whatever can contribute to the unity of all who believe in Christ: and to strengthen those aspects of the Church which can help to summon all of mankind into her embrace." In drafting the Constitution, Father Bugnini clearly envisaged the liturgy as a means of promoting ecumenism. (See his comment on pp. 58-59 below.) It follows from this that the traditional Roman Mass, which emphasized precisely those aspects of our Faith most unacceptable to Protestants, must be considered as hampering ecumenism. In order to promote ecumenism, radical reform would be necessary.

There had, of course, been liturgical development in the past within the Roman Rite, as in all rites, but this had taken place by a scarcely perceptible process of natural development. In his Introduction to the French edition of

---

64. *Ibid.*, pp. 124-125.
65. R. Kaiser, *Inside the Council* (London: Burns & Oates, 1963), p. 222.

The Reform of the Roman Liturgy by Msgr. Klaus Gamber, Cardinal Ratzinger wrote:

> J. A. Jungmann, one of the truly great liturgists of our time, defined the liturgy of his day, such as it could be understood in the light of historical research, as a "liturgy which is the fruit of development" . . . What happened after the Council was something else entirely: in the place of the liturgy as the fruit of development came fabricated liturgy. We abandoned the organic, living process of growth and development over centuries and replaced it, as in a manufacturing process, with a fabrication, a banal on-the-spot product (*produit banal de l'instant*).[66]

It is important to note that the predominant characteristic of this natural development was the addition of new prayers and gestures which manifested ever more clearly the mystery enshrined in the Mass. The Protestant Reformers removed prayers which made Catholic doctrine specific, under the guise of an alleged return to primitive simplicity. Pope Pius XII specifically condemned "certain attempts to reintroduce ancient rites and liturgies" on the grounds that they were primitive. In his encyclical *Mediator Dei* he wrote:

> The desire to restore everything indiscriminately to its ancient condition is neither wise nor praiseworthy. It would be wrong, for example, to want the altar restored to its ancient form of a table; to want black eliminated from liturgical colors, and pictures and statues eliminated from our churches; to require crucifixes that do not represent the bitter sufferings of the divine Redeemer; to condemn polyphonic chants, even though they conform to the regulations of the Apostolic See . . . This attitude is an attempt to revive the "archaeologism" to which the pseudo-synod of Pistoia gave rise; it seeks also to re-introduce the pernicious errors which led to that synod and resulted from it and which the

---

66. Introduction by Cardinal Ratzinger to *La Réforme Liturgique en question* (Le Barroux: Éditions Sainte-Madeleine), 1992, pp. 7-8.

Church, in her capacity of watchful guardian of "the Deposit of Faith" entrusted to her by her divine Founder, has rightly condemned. It is a wicked movement that tends to paralyze the sanctifying and salutary action by which the liturgy leads the children of adoption on the path to their heavenly Father. (Pars. 66-68).

The liturgical principles of Pistoia, one of which will be explained below, have been imposed throughout the Roman Rite as part of the conciliar reform, even though not specifically ordered by the Council. The CSL provided the door through which they entered.

Since the Second Vatican Council, tabernacles throughout the English-speaking world have been removed from their rightful place of honor in the center of the high altar. There is not one word in the CSL that even hints at this deplorable practice. It was, however, part of the program of the "young wolves" of the Liturgical Movement, and Pope Pius XII was well aware of this. The great Pontiff made his position on the tabernacle clear in an address to a liturgical congress in Assisi in 1956. He insisted that those who clung wholeheartedly to the teaching of the Council of Trent would have "no thought of formulating objections against the presence of the tabernacle on the altar." He had no doubt as to the true motivation of those seeking to change the traditional practice: "There is question, not so much of the material presence of the tabernacle on the altar, as of a tendency to which we would like to call your attention, that of a lessening of esteem for the presence and action of Christ in the tabernacle." This holy Pontiff then summed up the authentic Catholic position in one profound and perceptive sentence: "To separate tabernacle from altar is to separate two things which by their origin and nature should remain united." If this was true in 1956, it is still true today.[67]

---

67. A detailed history of the post-Vatican II campaign to remove the tabernacle from the high altar is provided in my booklet *The Catholic Sanctuary and the Second Vatican Council* (Rockford, IL: TAN, 1997).

It is worth pointing out that the "circumstances and needs of modern times," which Article 4 of the CSL claims that the liturgy must be adjusted to meet, have occurred with great regularity throughout history. It is of the nature of time to become more modern with the passing of each second, and if the Church had adapted the liturgy to keep up with the constant succession of modern times and new circumstances, there would never have been any liturgical stability at all. If this need for adaptation of the liturgy does exist, it must always have existed. The corpus of papal teaching on the liturgy is readily available, but papal teaching on the need to adapt the liturgy to keep pace with modern times is conspicuous only by its absence—and this is hardly surprising when this alleged "need" is examined in a dispassionate and rational manner. When do times become modern? How long do they remain modern? What are the criteria by which modernity is assessed? When does one modernity cease and another modernity come into being?

The complete fallacy of this "adaptation-to-modernity" thesis was certainly not lost upon some of the Council Fathers. Bishop (later Cardinal) Dino Staffa pointed out the theological consequences of an "adapted liturgy" on October 24, 1962. He told 2,337 assembled Fathers:

> It is said that the Sacred Liturgy must be adapted to times and circumstances which have changed. Here also we ought to look at the consequences. For customs, even the very face of society, change fast and will change even faster. What seems agreeable to the wishes of the multitude today will appear incongruous after thirty or fifty years. We must conclude then that after thirty or fifty years all, or almost all of the liturgy would have to be changed again. This seems to be logical according to the premises, this seems logical to me, but hardly fitting (*decorum*) for the Sacred Liturgy, hardly useful for the dignity of the Church, hardly safe for the integrity and unity of the faith, hardly favoring the unity of discipline. While the world therefore tends to unity more and more every day, especially in its manner of working or living, are we of the Latin Church going to break the admirable

liturgical unity and divide into nations, regions, even provinces?[68]

The answer, of course, is that this is precisely what the Latin Church was going to do and did—with the disastrous consequences for the integrity and unity both of faith and discipline which Bishop Staffa had foreseen.

Omission of the Term "Transubstantiation"

Articles 5 to 13 of the CSL, which deal with the nature of the liturgy, contain much admirable doctrinal teachings but also some which seem disturbingly lacking in precision. Christ's substantial presence in the Blessed Sacrament is referred to as if it is simply the highest (maximal) of His many presences in the liturgy, which includes His spiritual presence through the reading of Holy Scripture or through the fact that two or three are gathered together in His name. The CSL states only that Our Lord is present "especially under the Eucharistic species" (*Praesens . . . maxime sub speciebus eucharisticis*). (Article 7).

"Transubstantiation" is the classic Catholic term which the Church uses in order to express the Catholic teaching that in the Eucharist, the whole substance of the bread is converted into the substance of the Body of Christ, and the whole substance of the wine is converted into the substance of His Blood, with only the *appearances* of bread and wine remaining.

One fact which is made very clear in my book *Cranmer's Godly Order* is that all the Protestant Reformers agreed that Christ was present in the Eucharist; what they rejected was the dogma of His *substantial* presence. If there is one word which was and is anathema to Protestants, it is the word "transubstantiation." Protestants will profess belief in Christ's "real presence," in His "eucharistic presence," in His "sacramental presence"—Lutherans even pro-

---

68. Kaiser, p. 130.

fess belief in His "consubstantial presence"—but what they will not accept, what is anathema to them, is the one word "transubstantiation." It is, therefore, astonishing to find that this word does not appear anywhere within the text of the CSL. This is a scarcely credible break with the tradition of the Catholic and Roman Church, which has always insisted on absolute precision when writing of the Sacrament which is her greatest treasure, for it is nothing less than God Incarnate Himself.

The contrast between the traditional precision of the Church and the CSL can be made clear with just one example. Compared to the wording of the CSL, the following would *seem* to be an extremely comprehensive definition of Christ's Eucharistic presence: "Christ is, after the Consecration, truly, really and substantially present under the appearances of bread and wine, and the whole substance of bread and wine has then ceased to exist, only the appearances remaining." Readers will be surprised to learn that this definition was condemned by the Church as "pernicious, derogatory to the expounding of Catholic truth about the dogma of transubstantiation, favorable to heretics (*perniciosa, derogans expositioni veritatis catholicae circa dogma transsubstantiationis, favens haereticis*)." This definition was, in fact, the definition put forward by the Jansenist Synod of Pistoia; it was condemned by Pope Pius VI specifically for its calculated omission of the doctrine of transubstantiation and of the term "transubstantiation," which had been used by the Council of Trent (1545-1563) in defining the manner of Christ's Eucharistic presence and in the solemn profession of faith subscribed to by the Fathers of that Council ("*quam velut articulum fidei Tridentinum Concilium definivit* [v. n. 877, 884], *et quae in solemni fidei professione continetur* [v. n. 997]").[69] The failure to utilize the word "transubstantiation" was condemned by Pope Pius VI "inasmuch as, through an unauthorized and suspicious omission of this kind, mention is omitted of

---

69. H. Denzinger, *Enchiridion Symbolorum* (31ˢᵗ edition), No. 1529.

an article relating to the faith, and also of a word consecrated by the Church to safeguard the profession of that article against heresy, and because it tends to result in its being forgotten, as if it were merely a scholastic question."[70]

While discussing this particular point, it is impossible not to note what could be described as the truly supernatural correspondence between what Pope Pius VI wrote in 1794 and what Pope Paul VI wrote in his encyclical *Mysterium Fidei* in 1965. This encyclical aroused considerable hostility among both Protestants and liberal Catholics, who did not hesitate to stigmatize it as incompatible with the "spirit" of Vatican II!

A Protestant Observer mentioned earlier, Dr. Robert McAfee Brown, complained:

> On the eve of the fourth session he [Paul VI] issued an encyclical on the Eucharist, *Mysterium Fidei*, that seemed to most interpreters to be at best a backward looking document and at the worst a repudiation of many of the creative insights of the already promulgated constitution *On the Sacred Liturgy*.[71]

The encyclical *Mysterium Fidei* was, to quote another Protestant Observer, the Anglican Dr. J. Moorman, "disappointing to those who felt that the Council was really trying to break away from medieval scholasticism and Tridentine theology and speak to the modern world in language which it could understand."[72] The ultra-liberal *peritus* Father Gregory Baum, a convert from Judaism, commented: "Since Pope Paul's terminology is so different from the Constitution on the Liturgy, it is not easy to fit his encyclical harmoniously into the conciliar teaching of Vatican II."[73] A few quotations from *Mysterium Fidei* will make it clear why the

---

70. *Ibid.*
71. Robert McAfee Brown, *Ecumenical Revolution*, pp. 171-172.
72. J. Moorman, *Vatican Observed* (London: Darton, Longman & Tod, 1967), p. 157.
73. *Herder Correspondence*, 1965, p. 359.

encyclical was considered by liberals to be a terribly retrograde statement of Catholic dogma. Pope Paul condemned certain opinions that were current during the Council:

> Such opinions relate to Masses celebrated privately, to the dogma of transubstantiation and to eucharistic worship. They seem to think that although a doctrine has been defined once by the Church, it is open to anyone to ignore it or to give it an interpretation that whittles away the natural meaning of the words or the accepted sense of the concepts.

The Church teaches us, the Pope insists, that our blessed Lord "becomes present in the sacrament precisely by a marvellous change of the bread's whole substance into His Body and of the wine's whole substance into His Blood. This is clearly a remarkable and singular change, and the Catholic Church gives it the suitable and accurate name of transubstantiation."

Pope John XXIII had stated in his opening speech to the Council: "The substance of the ancient doctrine of the deposit of faith is one thing, and the way in which it is presented is another." Pope Paul VI appears to differ from his predecessor when he writes:

> This rule of speech has been introduced by the Church in the long run of centuries with the protection of the Holy Spirit. She has confirmed it with the authority of the Councils. It has become more than once the token and standard of orthodox faith. It must be observed religiously. No one may presume to alter it at will, or on the pretext of new knowledge. For it would be intolerable if the dogmatic formulas which ecumenical Councils have employed in dealing with the mysteries of the most holy Trinity were to be accused of being badly attuned to the men of our day, and other formulas were rashly introduced to replace them. It is equally intolerable that anyone on his own initiative should want to modify the formulas with which the Council of Trent has proposed the Eucharistic mystery for belief. These formulas, and others too, which the Church employs in proposing dog-

mas of faith, express concepts which are not tied to any specified cultural system. They are not restricted to any fixed development of the sciences nor to one or other of the theological schools.

Not withstanding the deplorable absence of the term *transubstantiation* from the CSL, Articles 5 to 13 do contain much orthodox teaching, teaching which must have gone a long way toward prompting conservative Fathers to vote for the Constitution and diverting attention from the time bombs in the text. The Council of Trent is quoted to the effect that "The victory and triumph of Christ's death are again made present" whenever the Mass is offered (Art. 6), and it is quoted again in stating that the Mass is offered by Christ: "the same one now offering through the ministry of priests, who formerly offered Himself on the cross." (Art. 7). "Rightly then is the liturgy considered as an exercise of the priestly office of Jesus Christ." (Art. 7). It is "the summit toward which all the activity of the Church is directed; at the same time it is the fountain from which all her power flows." (Art. 10).

Active Participation

In Article 11 there appears one of the key themes of the CSL. Pastors of souls are urged to ensure that during the Mass "the faithful take part knowingly, actively, and fruitfully." Similar admonitions are included in Pope Pius XII's *Mediator Dei* (1947), but in both that encyclical and in the CSL the Latin word which has been translated as "active" is *actuosus*. There is a Latin word *activus* which is defined in Lewis and Short's *Latin Dictionary* as active, practical, opposed to *contemplativus*, but the same dictionary explains *actuosus* as implying activity with the accessory idea of zeal, subjective impulse. It is not easy to provide an exact English equivalent of *actuosus*; the word involves a sincere (perhaps intense) interior participation in the Mass—and it is always to this interior participation that

prime consideration must be given. The role of external gestures is to manifest this interior participation, without
which they are totally without value. These signs should not
only manifest, but aid the interior participation which they
symbolize.

No gesture approved by the Church is without meaning
and value—the striking of the breast during the *Confiteor*,
making the Sign of the Cross on the forehead, lips and heart
at the beginning of the Gospel, genuflecting at the *Incarnatus est* during the Creed and at the *Verbum caro factum est*
of the Last Gospel, kneeling for certain parts of the Mass—
the Canon in particular, bowing in adoration at the eleva-
tions, joining in the chants and appropriate responses: all
these are appropriate external manifestations of the inter-
nal participation which the faithful should rightly be
taught to make knowingly and fruitfully. But Pope Pius XII
points out in *Mediator Dei* that the importance of this external participation should not be exaggerated and that every
Catholic has the right to assist at Mass in the manner
which he finds most helpful:

> People differ so widely in character, temperament and
> intelligence that it is impossible for them all to be affected in
> the same way by the same communal prayers, hymns, and
> sacred actions. Besides, spiritual needs and dispositions are
> not the same in all, nor do these remain unchanged in the
> same individual at different times. Are we therefore to say—
> as we should have to say if such an opinion were true—that
> all these Christians are unable to take part in the Eucharis-
> tic Sacrifice or to enjoy its benefits? Of course they can, and
> in ways which many find easier: for example, by devoutly
> meditating on the mysteries of Jesus Christ, or by perform-
> ing other religious exercises and saying other prayers which,
> though different in form from the liturgical prayers, are by
> their nature in keeping with them. (Par. 115).

As Pope Pius XII explains at great length in his encyclical, what really matters is that the faithful should unite
themselves with the priest at the altar in offering Christ

and should offer themselves together with the Divine Victim, with and through the great High Priest Himself. This is "participation" of the highest kind in the Mass.

There is a clear change of emphasis between *Mediator Dei* (1947) and the CSL (1964), which states that "in the restoration and promotion of the sacred liturgy, the full and active participation by all the people is the aim to be considered before all else, for it is the primary and indispensable source from which the faithful are to derive the true Christian spirit." (Art. 14). As is the case in this quotation, *actuosus* has been translated invariably by the word "active," which is interpreted in its literal sense. The necessity of making, as Article 14 directs, full and active congregational participation the prime consideration in "the restoration and promotion of the sacred liturgy" has resulted in the congregation rather than the Divine Victim becoming the focus of attention. Since the Council, it is the coming together of the community which matters most, not the reason they come together; and this is in harmony with the most obvious tendency within the post-conciliar Church—to replace the cult of God with the cult of man. Cardinal Ratzinger remarked with great perceptiveness in 1997:

> I am convinced that the crisis in the Church that we are experiencing is to a large extent due to the disintegration of the liturgy . . . when the community of faith, the worldwide unity of the Church and her history, and the mystery of the living Christ are no longer visible in the liturgy, where else, then, is the Church to become visible in her spiritual essence? Then the community is celebrating only itself, an activity that is utterly fruitless.[74]

Once the logic of making the active participation of the congregation the prime consideration of the liturgy is accepted, there can be no restraint upon the self-appointed

---

74. Joseph Ratzinger, *Milestones* (San Francisco: Ignatius Press, 1998), pp. 148-149.

experts intent upon its total desacralization.

It is important to stress here that at no time during the reform have the wishes of the laity ever been taken into consideration. Just as in the Soviet Union the Communist Party "interpreted the will of the people," so the "experts" interpret the wishes of the laity. When, as early as March 1964, members of the laity in England were making it quite clear that they neither liked nor wanted the liturgical changes being imposed upon them, one of England's most fervent apostles of liturgical innovation, Dom Gregory Murray, O.S.B., put them in their place in the clearest possible terms in a letter to *The Tablet*: "The plea that the laity as a body do not want liturgical change, whether in rite or in language, is, I submit, quite beside the point." He insists that it is "not a question of what people want; it is a question of what is good for them."[75] The self-appointed liturgical experts treat with complete contempt not only the laity, but also the parish clergy—whose bishops insist that they submit to the diktat of these experts, to whom, in most cases, they have abdicated their authority in liturgical matters. Monsignor Richard J. Schuler, an experienced parish priest in St. Paul, Minnesota, explained the predicament of the parish clergy very clearly in an article written in 1978 in which he made the very poignant comment that all that the experts require them to do is to raise the money to pay for their own destruction:

> But then came the post-conciliar interpreters and implementors who invented the "Spirit of the Council." They introduced practices never dreamed of by the Council Fathers; they did away with Catholic traditions and customs never intended to be disturbed; they changed for the sake of change; they upset the sheep and terrified the shepherds.
>
> The parish priest, who is for most Catholics the shepherd to whom they look for help along the path to salvation, fell upon hard times after the pastoral council. He is the pastor, but he found himself superseded by commissions, commit-

---

75. *The Tablet*, March 14, 1964, p. 303.

tees, experts, consultants, co-ordinators, facilitators, and bureaucrats of every description. A mere parish priest can no longer qualify. He is told that if he was educated prior to 1963, then he is ignorant of needed professional knowledge, he must be updated, retread and indoctrinated by attending meetings, seminars, workshops, retreats, conferences and other brainwashing sessions. But down deep, he really knows that what he is needed for is only to collect the money to support the ever-growing bureaucracy that every diocese has sprouted to serve the "pastoral needs" of the people. While the parishes struggle, the taxation imposed on them all but crushes them. The anomaly of having to pay for one's own destruction becomes the plight of a pastor and his sheep who struggle to adapt to the "freedom" and the options given by the council.

Msgr. Schuler certainly agrees with Msgr. Gamber that the reform as we have it would not have been endorsed by the majority of the Council Fathers. He continues:

Not least among the blows received by a pastor and his flock have been the liturgical innovations imposed by the Washington bureaucracy. Most of the changes we have witnessed since 1965 were never dreamed of by the Conciliar Fathers, and hardly one of them was ever asked for by the Catholic people. But with the new given freedom, we must have options, and we *must* use options, particularly the options that the liturgists propose. The liberal position means that one is free to agree with the Liberal position and no other. Thus options, as they are introduced, soon become the norm, and any exercise of choice is soon labelled divisive.[76]

Pulling the Liturgy Down to Our Level

The demand that the full and active participation of the congregation "be considered before all else" is a time bomb of virtually unlimited destructive power placed in the hands

---

76. *The Wanderer*, November 2, 1978.

of those invested with the power to implement in practice the details of a reform which the Council authorized, but did not spell out in detail. Thus, although the Council says that "other things being equal," Gregorian chant should be given pride of place in liturgical services (Art. 116), the "experts" can and did argue that this was most certainly not a case of other things being equal, as the use of Gregorian chant impeded the active participation of the people. The music of the people, popular music, pop music, is, say the "experts," clearly what is most pleasing to them and most likely to promote their active participation—which, in obedience to the Council, must "be considered before all else." This has led to the abomination of the "Folk Mass," which certainly has no more in common with genuine folk music than it does with plainchant. It also illustrates the ignorance of, and contempt for, the ordinary faithful that is manifested by these self-styled "experts." Because the housewife or the manual laborer listens to pop music to relieve the monotony of the day's routine, it does not follow that they are incapable of appreciating anything better, or that they wish to hear the same sort of music in Church on Sunday. The same is equally true of young people: if the liturgy is reduced to the level of imitating what was being heard in the disco last year, then the young will soon see little point in being present. Dietrich von Hildebrand has correctly defined the issue at stake as follows:

> The basic error of most of the innovators is to imagine that the new liturgy brings the holy Sacrifice of the Mass nearer to the faithful, that shorn of its old rituals the Mass now enters into the substance of our lives. For the question is whether we better meet Christ in the Mass by soaring up to Him, or by dragging Him down into our own pedestrian, workaday world. The innovators would replace holy intimacy with Christ by an unbecoming familiarity. The new liturgy actually threatens to frustrate the confrontation with Christ, for it discourages reverence in the face of mystery, precludes awe, and all but extinguishes a sense of sacredness. What really matters, surely, is not whether the

faithful feel at home at Mass, but whether they are drawn out of their ordinary lives into the world of Christ—whether their attitude is the response of ultimate reverence: whether they are imbued with the reality of Christ.[77]

Professor von Hildebrand issued this warning against the clear direction which the liturgical reform was taking in 1966, a direction in which it was being steered by "experts" claiming that they knew the style of celebration which was necessary to ensure that the congregation could participate actively—and this, they could point out, was what the Council had decreed must "be considered before all else." Professor von Hildebrand denounces this attitude in very severe terms:

> They seem to be unaware of the elementary importance of sacredness in religion. Thus, they dull the sense of the sacred and thereby undermine true religion. Their "democratic" approach makes them overlook the fact that in all men who have a longing for God there is also a longing for the sacred and a sense of difference between the sacred and the profane. The worker or peasant has this sense as much as any intellectual. If he is a Catholic, he will desire to find a sacred atmosphere in the church, and this remains true whether the world is urban, industrial or not. . . . Many priests believe that replacing the sacred atmosphere that reigns, for example, in the marvellous churches of the Middle Ages or the baroque epoch, and in which the Latin Mass was celebrated, with a profane, functionalist, neutral, humdrum atmosphere will enable the Church to encounter the simple man in charity. But this is a fundamental error. It will not fulfill his deepest longing; it will merely offer him stones for bread. Instead of combatting the irreverence so widespread today these priests are actually helping to propagate this irreverence.[78]

---

77. *Triumph* magazine, October 1966.
78. D. von Hildebrand, *Trojan Horse in the City of God* (Chicago: Franciscan Herald Press, 1969), p. 135.

A Permanently Evolving Liturgy

The next time bomb is located in Article 21. It states that "the liturgy is made up of unchangeable elements divinely instituted and elements subject to change." This is perfectly correct—but it does not follow that, because certain elements could be changed, they ought to be changed. The entire liturgical tradition of the Roman rite contradicts such an assertion. "What we may call the 'archaisms' of the Missal," writes Dom Cabrol, a "father" of the liturgical movement, "are the expressions of the faith of our fathers which it is our duty to watch over and hand on to posterity."[79] Similarly, in their defense of the bull *Apostolicae Curae* (1898), the Catholic Bishops of the Province of Westminster insisted that:

> In adhering rigidly to the rite handed down to us we can always feel secure . . . And this sound method is that which the Catholic Church has always followed . . . to subtract prayers and ceremonies in previous use, and even to remodel the existing rites in the most drastic manner, is a proposition for which we know of no historical foundation, and which appears to us absolutely incredible. Hence Cranmer in taking this unprecedented course acted, in our opinion, with the most inconceivable rashness.[80]

The CSL takes a different view, so startling and unprecedented a break with tradition that it seems scarcely credible that the Council Fathers voted for it. Article 21 states that elements which are subject to change "not only may but ought to be changed with the passing of time if features have by chance crept in which are less harmonious with the intimate nature of the liturgy, or if existing elements have grown less functional." These norms are so vague that the scope for interpreting them is virtually limitless, and it

---

79. Introduction to the Cabrol edition of *The Roman Missal.*
80. *A Vindication of the Bull "Apostolicae Curae"* (London: Longmans, Green & Co., 1898), pp. 42-3.

must be kept in mind continually that those who drafted them would be the men with the power to interpret them. No indication is given of which aspects of the liturgy are referred to here; no indication is given of the meaning of "less functional" (how much less is "less"?), or whether "functional" refers to the original function or a new one which may have been acquired.

Article 21 refers, of course, to the liturgy in general, but specific reference is made to the Mass in Article 50:

> The rite of the Mass is to be revised in such a way that the intrinsic nature and purpose of its several parts, as also the connection between them, can be more clearly manifested, and that devout and active participation by the faithful can be more easily accomplished. For this purpose the rites are to be simplified, while due care is taken to preserve their substance. Elements which, with the passage of time, came to be duplicated, or were added with but little advantage are now to be discarded. Where opportunity allows or necessity demands, other elements which have suffered injury through the accidents of history are now to be restored to the earlier norm of the holy Fathers.

Those who have read my book *Cranmer's Godly Order* will be struck immediately by the fact that Thomas Cranmer himself could have written this passage as the basis for his own "reform" of the Catholic liturgy—i.e., his creation of the Anglican prayer service. There is not one point here that the apostate Archbishop of Canterbury (1489-1556) did not claim to be implementing. An Anglican observer at Vatican II, Archdeacon Bernard Pawley, praised the manner in which the liturgical reform following Vatican II not only corresponds with, but has even surpassed, the reform of Thomas Cranmer.[81] There is a very close correspondence between the prayers which Cranmer felt had been added to the Mass "with little advantage" (almost invariably prayers

---

81. B. Pawley, *Rome and Canterbury through Four Centuries* (London: Mowbray, 1974), p. 349.

which made Catholic teaching explicit) and those which the members of the *Consilium*, which implemented the norms of Vatican II (with the help of Protestant advisers), also decreed had been added "with little advantage" and must "be discarded." The correspondence between the reform of Thomas Cranmer and those of Father Bugnini's *Consilium* is made clear in Chapter XXV of my book *Pope Paul's New Mass*, where the two reforms are set out in parallel columns with the Traditional Latin Rite Mass codified in perpetuity by St. Pius V (1566-1572).

Article 21 of the CSL, together with such Articles as 1, 23, 50 and 62, have served as a mandate for the supreme goal of the liturgical revolutionaries—that of a permanently evolving liturgy. In September 1968 the bulletin of the Archdiocese of Paris, *Présence et Dialogue*, called for a permanent revolution in these words: "It is no longer possible, in a period when the world is developing so rapidly, to consider rites as definitively fixed once and for all. They need to be regularly revised." This is precisely the consequence which Bishop Staffa had warned at Vatican Council II would be inevitable, in the 1962 speech cited above. (Pp. 30-31). Once the logic of Article 21 is accepted, there can be no alternative to a permanently evolving liturgy.

The Council *periti* established the journal *Concilium,* which was to all intents and purposes their official mouthpiece (the journal should not be confused with the Commission, *Consilium*, which is spelled with an "s"). Cardinal Heenan remarked:

> The Ordinary Magisterium of the Pope is exercised in his writings and allocutions. But today what the Pope says is by no means accepted as authoritative by all Catholic theologians. An article in the periodical *Concilium* is at least as likely to win their respect as a papal encyclical. The decline of the Magisterium is one of the most significant developments in the post-conciliar Church.[82]

---

82. *The Tablet*, May 18, 1968.

The Cardinal made this comment in May 1968, and its accuracy was demonstrated dramatically and depressingly two months later when the encyclical *Humanae Vitae* (July 25, 1968) was rejected publicly and contemptuously by hundreds of Catholic theologians throughout the world who, in almost every case, retained their positions as official teachers of the Catholic Church. Writing in *Concilium* in 1969, Father H. Rennings, Dean of Studies of the Liturgical Institute of Trier, stated:

> When the Constitution states that one of the aims is "to adapt more suitably to the needs of our own times those institutions which are subject to change" (Art. 1; see also Arts. 21, 23, 62), it clearly expresses the dynamic elements in the Council's idea of the liturgy. The "needs of our time" can always be better understood and therefore demand other solutions; the needs of the next generation can again lead to other consequences for the way worship should operate and be fitted into the overall activity of the Church. The basic principle of the Constitution may be summarized as applying the principle of a Church which is constantly in a state of reform (*ecclesia semper reformanda*) to the liturgy which is always in the state of reform (*liturgia semper reformanda*). And the implied renewal must not be understood as limited to eliminating possible abuses but as that always necessary renewal of a Church endowed with all the potential that must lead to fullness and pluriformity. It is a mistake to think of liturgical reform as an occasional spring cleaning that settles liturgical problems for another period of rest.[83]

This could hardly be more explicit. It is clear that Cardinal Heenan was not speaking entirely in jest when he remarked:

> There is a certain poetic justice in the humiliation of the Catholic Church at the hands of liturgical anarchists. Catholics used to laugh at Anglicans for being "high" or

83. *Concilium*, February 1971, p. 64.

"low". . . The old boast that the Mass is everywhere the same and that Catholics are happy whichever priest celebrates is no longer true. When on December 7, 1962 the bishops voted overwhelmingly (1,922 against 11) in favour of the first chapter of the Constitution on the Liturgy, they did not realize that they were initiating a process which after the Council would cause confusion and bitterness throughout the Church.[84]

Father Joseph Gelineau was described by Archbishop Bugnini as one of the "great masters of the international liturgical world."[85] In his book *Demain la liturgie*, Father Gelineau informs us that:

> It would be false to identify this liturgical renewal with the reform of rites decided on by Vatican II. This reform goes back much further and goes forward far beyond the conciliar prescriptions (*elle va bien au-delà*). The liturgy is a permanent workshop (*la liturgie est un chantier permanent*).[86]

This concept of a permanently evolving liturgy—"the liturgy is a permanent workshop"—is of crucial importance. St. Pius V's ideal of liturgical uniformity within the Roman Rite has now been cast aside, to be replaced by an ideal of "pluriformity" in which the liturgy must be kept in a state of constant flux, resulting inevitably in what Cardinal Ratzinger described with perfect accuracy as "the disintegration of the liturgy."

Is Father Rennings' desire for a *liturgia semper reformanda*—"liturgy always to be reformed"—a legitimate interpretation of the CSL? When he speaks of "the Council's idea of the liturgy," he means, of course, the idea of the Bugnini Commission, which drafted the CSL, and of the Bugnini *Consilium,* which was officially charged with

---

84. Heenan, p. 367.

85. Bugnini, p. 221.

86. J. Gelineau, *Demain la liturgie* (Paris: Les Editions du Cerf, 1977), pp. 9-10.

implementing it. In practice this comes down to the same thing, one could even say to the same person: Father Bugnini. As secretary to the *Consilium,* he was thus able to utilize the time bombs that he had inserted into his draft *schema* precisely as he had intended to use them, to impose radical changes not intended by Pope John XXIII and the bishops who voted for the CSL.

Instruction Overshadows Worship

Another time bomb is contained in Article 33: "Although the sacred liturgy is above all things the worship of the divine Majesty, it likewise contains abundant instruction for the faithful." Take careful note of the word "although." The essential nature of the liturgy as a solemn act of worship offered to the Eternal Father seems to be safeguarded—but on a practical level, little more is heard of "the worship of the divine Majesty," but a great deal is heard about the "abundant instruction of the faithful." As was mentioned earlier, the tragedy of the Liturgical Movement was the fact that it would make this secondary aspect of the liturgy the primary aspect.

For the Protestant, it is the written word of the Bible which is of paramount importance in worship; it is to receive this written word in readings and preaching and to respond by praising God in prayers and hymns that Protestants come together. On the other hand, the Catholic assists at Mass primarily by offering, adoring and then receiving the Incarnate Word Himself. Those wishing to change the Mass in the interests of ecumenical convergence have been able to utilize Article 33 to add considerable emphasis to the instructional part of the Mass, while the prominence given to the sacrifice has been considerably diminished. Xavier Rynne, who wrote for the *New Yorker*, notes with satisfaction that the CSL

> establishes the function of the Word of God in liturgical worship, placing the emphasis on Scripture as understood by

modern biblical theology, and thereby furnishing a realistic
bridge for a dialogue with the Protestant Churches whose
worship has always been biblically rather than sacramen-
tally orientated.[87]

Rynne's conclusion conforms perfectly with what was
explained on page 3 of this book: the tragedy of the Liturgical Movement was that it would make the pedagogical, or
educative aspect of the liturgy the primary aspect.

Article 34 of the CSL states that the reformed liturgy
must be "distinguished by a noble simplicity." There is,
needless to say, no attempt to explain precisely what constitutes "a noble simplicity." The liturgy must be "short"—
but *how* short? It must be "unencumbered by useless
repetitions"—but when does a repetition become useless?
(The very dreary repetitions in the New Mass which have
been introduced in the Responsorial Psalm and the Bidding
Prayers [Prayer of the Faithful] are therefore presumably
useful repetitions.) Article 34 also insists that the new rites
must "be within the people's powers of comprehension."
What is meant here by the word "people"? University grad-
uates, the illiterate, or those in the middle? Must anything
that anyone cannot comprehend be excluded? The latitude
which this article gave to the *Consilium* hardly needs
elaborating.

Article 37 claims that "the Church has no wish to impose
a rigid uniformity on matters which do not involve the faith
or the good of the whole community." It explains that anything in the way of life of various races and peoples that "is
not indissolubly bound up with superstition and error she
[the Church] studies with sympathy and, if possible, pre-
serves intact. Sometimes, in fact, she admits such things
into the liturgy itself, as long as they harmonize with its
true and authentic spirit." In practical terms this has meant
unrestricted pluriformity—with one exception. And in this
case the most rigid uniformity prevails in the overwhelming

---

87. X. Rynne, *The Second Session* (London: Herder & Herder, 1964), p. 305.

majority of dioceses in the Western world. This is the rigid uniformity of not allowing the Traditional Latin ("Tridentine") Mass codified by St. Pius V, despite the appeal to the bishops of the world by Pope John Paul II in his *motu proprio "Ecclesia Dei"* of July 11, 1988:

> To all those Catholic faithful who feel attached to some previous liturgical and disciplinary forms of the Latin tradition, I wish to manifest my will to facilitate their ecclesial communion by means of the necessary measures to guarantee respect for their rightful aspirations. In this matter I ask for the support of the bishops and of all those engaged in the pastoral ministry in the Church . . . moreover, respect must everywhere be shown for the feelings of all those who are attached to the Latin liturgical tradition, by a wide and generous application of the directives already issued some time ago by the Apostolic See, for the use of the Roman Missal according to the typical edition of 1962.

The Holy Father could hardly have made his will more clear, but such is the lack of respect for the Pope by the overwhelming majority of the world's bishops—and what can be described only too accurately as their hatred for tradition—that Mass according to the Missal of 1962 (i.e., the Traditional Latin Mass, also called the Tridentine Mass) is permitted by them in far less than one per cent of Catholic parishes of the Roman Rite throughout the world; and even where the bishops authorize such celebrations, these are sometimes scheduled for an inconvenient location at an inconvenient time, and only once a month or once a quarter, and often not even on Sunday. In point of fact, according to the 1986 Commission of Cardinals set up to examine the working of the 1984 indult *Quattuor abhinc annos*, no priest of the Roman Rite needs permission to use the 1962 Missal when celebrating Mass in Latin.[88]

---

88. See Appendix III.

Protestantism and the Mass

The Traditional Mass would appear to be the one thing in the way of life of so many Catholic peoples around the world that is so "bound up with superstition and error" that almost all bishops consider that it cannot be admitted to the liturgy. This has historically been the unanimous view of every Protestant sect—but some now take a very different view where the "reformed liturgy" is concerned.

The ultra-evangelical Church of the Confession of Augsburg/Alsace-Lorraine issued a statement after the meeting of its Superior Consistory on December 8, 1973, permitting its members to receive Holy Communion in Catholic churches: "We attach great importance to the use of the new prayers [of the Catholic liturgy], with which we feel at home, and which have the advantage of giving a different interpretation to the theology of sacrifice than we were accustomed to attribute to Catholicism. These prayers invite us to recognize an evangelical theology of sacrifice."[89] Dr. M. G. Siegvalt, a professor of dogmatic theology in the Protestant faculty at the University of Strasbourg, testified that "Nothing in the renewed Mass need really trouble an evangelical protestant."[90] The Protestant theologian Roger Mehl wrote in the September 10, 1970 issue of *Le Monde:*

> If one takes account of the decisive evolution in the Eucharistic liturgy of the Catholic Church, of the option of substituting other Eucharistic prayers for the Canon of the Mass, of the expunging of the idea that the Mass is a sacrifice, and of the possibility of receiving Communion under both kinds, then there is no further justification for the Reformed Churches' forbidding their members to assist at the Eucharist in a Catholic Church.

An Anglican bishop, Dr. John Moorman, remarked: "In reading the *schema* on the Liturgy, and in listening to the

---

89. *L'Église en Alsace*, January 1974.
90. *Le Monde*, November 22, 1969.

debate on it, I could not help thinking that, if the Church of Rome went on improving the Missal and Breviary long enough, they would one day triumphantly invent the Book of Common Prayer."[91] The justice of Dr. Moorman's observation can be demonstrated by noting the principal differences that would have been noticed before Vatican II between the Catholic Mass and a Protestant Communion Service:

1. *The Catholic Mass*—Latin. *Protestant Communion Service*—vernacular.
2. *Catholic*—much of the liturgy inaudible. *Protestant*—the entire service audible.
3. *Catholic*—only two readings. *Protestant*—generally three readings.
4. *Catholic*—no lay readers. *Protestant*—lay readers used.
5. *Catholic*—clearly performing solemn rites upon an altar facing the East. *Protestant*—a meal served upon a table, often facing the congregation. (The celebration of Mass *facing the people* is a pure innovation and a complete break with Catholic tradition in both the Roman and Eastern Rites. It is not mandated, recommended or even mentioned in Vatican II's Constitution on the Sacred Liturgy. See *The Catholic Sanctuary and the Second Vatican Council.*)
6. *Catholic*—kneeling throughout long periods of the service, particularly for the reception of Communion. *Protestant*—little kneeling; Communion often received standing.
7. *Catholic*—the people receive Holy Communion on the tongue. *Protestant*—Communion given in the hand.
8. *Catholic*—Communion received only under one kind. *Protestant*—Communion received under both kinds.
9. *Catholic*—frequent liturgical reference to the doctrines of sacrifice and Real Presence. *Protestant*—no reference whatsoever to the offering of any sacrifice beyond that of the congregation offering itself. Some references to the Body and Blood of Christ which could give the impression of belief in the Real Presence.

---

91. Moorman, p. 47.

A Ban on Kneeling for Holy Communion

Not one of these differences would be apparent in a typical Catholic parish celebration in the United States today. As regards No. 6, standing for Communion, at the end of 2002 the Bishops' Conference of the United States decreed, apparently in deference to the principle of a permanently evolving liturgy, that the faithful must stand for the reception of Holy Communion. Decisions of an episcopal conference are not binding on individual bishops, but even relatively conservative bishops such as Archbishop Charles Chaput of Denver bowed to the conference, which in its turn had kow-towed to its so-called liturgical experts, its *periti*, in imposing this diktat. The February 5, 2003 edition of the *Denver Catholic Register* carried an exhortation of almost heroic banality from the Archbishop:

> In the revised *General Instruction on the Roman Missal*, the Holy See indicated that uniformity of gesture should be respected at this time in a specific way. The specific gesture was to be determined by the appropriate conference of bishops, and this has been done in the United States. The bishops have determined that we should not kneel or genuflect. We receive Communion standing. Before receiving, we bow our head in adoration, and we say "Amen" and receive the body of Christ on the tongue or in the hand. This will be new for many of the faithful, because the formal act of reverence was not widely promoted in the past. This act helps us avoid nonchalance in receiving holy Communion. It allows us to acknowledge what we are about to do: take under the form of bread and wine the resurrected body and blood of Christ. If we have become distracted during the procession, the gesture helps us to recollect ourselves. While the act of reverence will be new for some, it may be "different" for others. In the past, we may have made a sign of the cross, a profound bow (one from the waist), genuflected or simply knelt as our act of adoration. The Church now asks us to submit our personal preference to her wisdom. Some of us will need time to remember to do this. Others may not want to change the gesture of reverence they've been using. In all cases, we need to defer to the Church.

I have rarely seen so many *non sequiturs* in so short a space. If standing helps us avoid nonchalance in receiving Holy Communion, does kneeling promote nonchalance? If standing allows us to acknowledge that we are about to take under the form of bread and wine the resurrected Body and Blood of Christ, does kneeling preclude such acknowledgement? If standing helps us to recollect ourselves, does kneeling preclude recollection? The Archbishop informs us that "the act of reverence will be new for some." What utter nonsense! Standing is not an act of reverence, and has never been an act of reverence. He would profit from reading an article by Father Regis Scanlon, O.F.M., in the August-September 1994 issue of *Homiletic and Pastoral Review*. The Franciscan theologian reminds us:

> There is a good reason why the Church reserves the genuflection for its official act of reverence toward the Blessed Sacrament. Not just any act can be used for an act of adoration. For example, one could never use standing as an act of adoration in our culture nor in the oriental culture. We stand when a bishop or the President of the United States comes into the room, but we do not adore either one of them. Similarly, today, many bow at the presence of great dignitaries and human authority, but they do not adore them. This is also the case in oriental cultures today . . . the act of bending the knee before Jesus Christ is not just a relative act, or an act that is based purely on culture. Rather, it transcends culture because it is an act that has scriptural, traditional, and cosmic significance. God the Father says through Isaiah: "To me every knee shall bend" (Is. 45:23). And St. Paul says, "for it is written: 'As I live, says the Lord, every knee shall bend before me'" (Rom. 14:11). Again, St. Paul states: "at Jesus' name every knee must bend in the heavens, on the earth, and under the earth" (Phil. 2:10). And this "kneeling," or "bending of the knee," is the act of adoration of the Blessed Sacrament which has developed in the Tradition of the Church and which the faithful have adopted down through the ages. St. Francis of Assisi, for example, said in his twelfth century Letter to All Superiors of the Friars Minor: "When the priest is offering sacrifice at the altar or the

Blessed Sacrament is being carried about, everyone should kneel down and give praise, glory, and honour to our Lord and God, living and true."

Another Highly Destructive Time Bomb— "Legitimate Variations and Adaptations"

The principle enunciated in Article 37 of the CSL is expanded in Article 38 and constitutes a time bomb with a capacity for destruction almost equivalent to that of the principle of permanent liturgical evolution. "Provided that the substantial unity of the Roman rite is maintained, the revision of liturgical books should allow for legitimate variations and adaptations to different groups, regions, and peoples, especially in mission lands." (Excluding, of course, any group wishing to retain the Traditional Latin Mass codified by St. Pius V in 1570.) The mention of mission lands here is highly significant, as most Fathers would presume that this was where these adaptations would take place. However, the carefully worded text does not say "only," but "especially" in mission lands. Article 38 does indeed state that "the substantial unity of the Roman rite" is to be maintained—but what "substantial unity" means is not indicated. It would be for the *Consilium* to decide, and for the members of the *Consilium* (as for Humpty Dumpty), words mean whatever they want them to mean.[92]

Once this principle of adaptation has been accepted, there is no part of the Mass which can be considered exempt from change. Even the words of Consecration have been altered to bring them very close to the formula adopted by Thomas Cranmer in his reform.[93]

Article 38 by no means concludes the subject of adaptation. Without giving the least idea of what is meant by

---

92. "When *I* use a word," Humpty Dumpty said, in rather a scornful tone, "it means just what I choose it to mean — neither more nor less." (Lewis Carroll, *Through the Looking Glass*, Chapter VI).

93. M. Davies, *Cranmer's Godly Order* (Ft. Collins, CO: Roman Catholic Books, 1995 edition), Appendix III.

"legitimate variations and adaptations," the CSL goes on in Article 40 to state that in "some places and circumstances, however, an even more radical adaptation of the liturgy is needed." Without explaining what is meant by a "radical adaptation," the need for "an even more radical adaptation" is postulated! More radical than what? Once this bomb has exploded, the devastation it unleashes cannot be controlled. The Council Fathers, like Count Frankenstein, have given life to a creature which has a life and a will of its own and over which they have no power.

Liturgical Abuses Out of Control

As early as 1965, Cardinal Lercaro, head (or figurehead) of the *Consilium*, felt it necessary to send a letter to the bishops of the world begging them to stem the tide of unauthorized radical adaptations which endangered what he considered to be the sound official reform. He may have honestly failed to appreciate that these unofficial adaptations were simply the logical extension of the official radical adaptations enshrined in the articles of the CSL which have been cited. The *Consilium* was, the Cardinal assured the bishops, engaged in "a general reform of the liturgy which went right to its very foundations." Such a reform "could not be completed in one day." The new norms had been "conceived with a certain elasticity, which could permit adaptation, and in consequence great pastoral efficacy. That did not mean that every priest was free to devise whatever rites suited him." Cardinal Lercaro stated that he did not wish "the sense of fraternity, of a family assembled"—which had already made progress and needed to make even more—to stifle the "sense of hierarchy in the Church." Somehow or other the bishops needed to "put the brakes on arbitrary experiments, to this uncontrolled variety, and even the danger that the laity would . . . lament and murmur as did the sons of Israel against Moses and Aaron." He did not, of course, wish to imply that "unity consisted in stifling or eliminating variety"—he could hardly imply this, as the

CSL had called for variety and his own *Consilium* was already interpreting this call with a liberality far beyond anything the majority of Fathers would have dreamed possible. However, Cardinal Lercaro insisted that this variety should not be allowed to degenerate "into incoherence." The Cardinal begged for patience, urging the bishops to bring an end to the

> personal, premature, and noxious experiments, which God does not bless and which, in consequence, cannot result in lasting fruits; on the contrary, they injure the piety of the faithful and the renewal which has been so devoutly undertaken. They also prejudice our own efforts, for they are general, arbitrary initiatives, which finish by casting an unfavorable light on the work carried out with circumspection, a sense of responsibility, prudence and a true understanding of pastoral needs.[94]

Note that these startling admissions were made in 1965, and even by then the principle of a continually evolving, radically adapted, and legitimately varied liturgy was raging unrestrained throughout the Latin Church. Once again there is a striking similarity to Cranmer's reform, or in this instance, to the situation immediately prior to the introduction of the 1549 Prayer Book. In 16th-century England, numerous attacks upon traditional Eucharistic teaching were published, which the authorities reproved but took no effective steps to suppress. The King's Council issued orders restraining innovations in the liturgy, while letting it be known that such innovations were not unpleasing to them. The King, like Cardinal Lercaro, even found it necessary to issue a proclamation urging radical reformers "to stay and quiet themselves with this our direction—and not enterprise to run afore and so by their rashness to become the greatest hinderers" of change.[95]

The *Consilium*, as did the Council of King Edward VI,

---

94. *Notitiae*, Nos. 9-10, Sept.-Oct. 1965, p. 257 ff.
95. Cf. *Cranmer's Godly Order*, Chapter XI.

took little or no action against the "unofficial" innovators—indeed, how could it have done so? The official and unofficial innovators were on the same wavelength, in the same camp, pursuing the same objectives by converging routes. There was no disagreement on principle; there was no dispute that there should be continual evolution, adaptation and variety. The division on a matter of principle lay between the official and unofficial innovators on the one hand, and on the other hand the Traditionalists—who wished to retain the unity of the Roman Rite.

Legalize the Abuses!

Cardinal Lercaro's letter did nothing to halt the spread of "arbitrary initiatives." Rome adopted the tactic of bringing illicit innovations to an end by making them licit and official. Communion was given in the hand illicitly—let it be given in the hand officially! Communion was illicitly distributed by laymen—then appoint laymen as extraordinary ministers of Holy Communion. Those who considered that the essence of the Mass lies in its being a common meal began (not without logic) to receive Communion at more than one Mass on the same day—then let this be permitted in many circumstances. Priests began illicitly using *extempore* prayers—then let provision for *extempore* prayer be made within the official reform. Unofficial Eucharistic Prayers were composed—then let three new Eucharistic Prayers be provided. The composition of unofficial Eucharistic prayers continued—so add another five. Communion was given under both kinds at Sunday Mass in defiance of Vatican legislation—the practice was legalized, and so now it could not be claimed that the law concerning Communion under both kinds was being defied. Liturgical law was broken by allowing female acolytes into the sanctuary. Female acolytes were legalized, so the law permitting only male acolytes was no longer being broken—liturgical discipline had been restored!

The logic of this policy could not possibly be lost upon the unofficial innovators: let them introduce and spread their liturgical fantasies, and the Vatican would eventually legalize them. Even if Rome did not legalize the abuses, the possibility of action being taken against the unofficial innovators was remote in the extreme, particularly after the introduction of the New Mass in 1969. After that date, there were a few priests who "illicitly" continued to offer the Traditional Latin Mass, so those in the Vatican and elsewhere with a penchant for repression were able to find ample scope to indulge it by hounding these priests from their parishes.

Cardinal Lercaro's profession of "circumspection, a sense of responsibility, prudence and a true understanding of pastoral needs" takes on a very hollow ring now that the fruits of his official reform are available for anyone to see. These fruits were described in scathing but realistic terms by Monsignor Gamber:

> The liturgical reform, welcomed with so much idealism and hope by many priests and lay people alike, has turned out to be a liturgical destruction of startling proportions — a débâcle worsening with each passing year. Instead of the hoped-for renewal of the Church and of Catholic life, we are now witnessing a dismantling of the traditional values and piety on which our faith rests. Instead of the fruitful renewal of the liturgy, what we see is a destruction of the forms of the Mass which had developed organically during the course of many centuries.[96]

The time bombs inserted in the CSL have been exploded with a destructive power far beyond the extent that the revolutionaries who planted them there could have dared to hope. Their reverberations will continue to spread while there is anything left to which the name "official" can be attached. Father Bugnini was rewarded for his part in the reform with an Archbishop's mitre. He claimed in 1974— and who could dispute his claim—that "The liturgical

---

96. Gamber, p. 9.

reform is a major conquest of the Catholic Church, and it has ecumenical dimensions, since the other Churches and Christian denominations see in it not only something to be admired in itself, but equally as a sign of further progress to come."[97] As is always the case, every concession to revolutionaries is followed by new and more radical demands. It might have been imagined that by 1971 there had been enough variety and legitimate adaptation to suit everyone. Far from it! Writing in *Concilium,* Father Andrew Greeley, while deploring the "occasional madness" of the "underground" liturgy, considers the renewed liturgy to be "a creation of those who want in their liturgical experience more of what liturgical symbolism was originally intended to convey—that is, intimate and intense friendship." Among the examples of "occasional madness" cited by Father Greeley are the "marijuana mass, mass with crackers and whisky used as the elements for consecration, teen-age masses with Coca Cola and hot dog buns." However, the basic position of the participants in underground Masses is, claims Father Greeley, "unanswerable." He claims that "the underground is a judgment on us for our failure to understand the implications of the symbolism of the Eucharist as a family meal. If we do not provide a family meal for an increasing number of Catholics, then they will provide one for themselves."[98]

As a final example of a time bomb in the text of the CSL—it would become tedious to enumerate them all—the point must be made that while stating that the regulation of the liturgy is a responsibility reserved to the Apostolic See (Article 22), local ecclesiastical authorities are positively encouraged to propose any "adaptations" they deem necessary. (Article 40). They are reminded of the limitations of their powers of initiative, but the possibility of these powers being extended is more than implicit. (Articles 22 and 36). This has resulted in the hierarchies of such countries as France and Holland making themselves, for practical pur-

---

97. *Notitiae,* No. 92, April 1974, p. 126.
98. *Concilium,* February 1971, p. 66.

poses, the sole arbiters of what they will or will not allow—
which, again on a practical level, means that they will allow
anything but the Traditional Latin Mass. The Indian bishops, under the guise of inculturation, have, in fact, been
"Hinduizing" the Mass in their country. They have treated
with contempt the anguished protests of the laity; appeals
to Rome by the anguished laity have been ignored.

The Abolition of Latin

One apparently insurmountable obstacle to the revolution which the time bombs in the CSL were intended to initiate was the use of Latin in the liturgy. While the Latin
language remained the norm, there could in fact be no revolution. The Latin language has been, as Dom Guéranger
warned in his *Liturgical Institutions* (Vol. 1, ch. IV, 1840), a
principal target of the liturgical heretics:

> Hatred for the Latin language is inborn in the heart of all
> the enemies of Rome. They recognize it as the bond of
> Catholics throughout the universe, as the arsenal of ortho-
> doxy against all the subtleties of the sectarian spirit . . . We
> must admit it is a masterblow of Protestantism to have
> declared war on the sacred language. If it should ever suc-
> ceed in destroying it, it would be well on the way to victory.

Prophetic words indeed! The virtual abolition of the Latin
language from the Roman Rite was not only *not* intended by
the Council Fathers, but the possibility of this happening as
a result of the CSL would not have been taken seriously by
them had anyone suggested it. In this respect, at least, it
could seem that they had made their intentions explicit.
Article 36 states:

> 1. Particular law remaining in force, the use of the Latin
> language is to be preserved in the Latin rites.
> 2. But [and what an important "but" this is!] since the use
> of the mother tongue, whether in the Mass, the administra-
> tion of the sacraments, or other parts of the liturgy, may fre-

quently be of great advantage to the people, the limits of its employment may be extended. This extension will apply in the first place to the readings and directives, and to some of the prayers and chants, according to the regulations on this matter to be laid down separately in subsequent chapters.

3. It is for the competent territorial authority mentioned in Article 22.2 to decide whether, and to what extent, the vernacular language is to be used according to these norms; their decrees are to be approved, that is, confirmed, by the Apostolic See. And, whenever the procedure seems to be called for, this authority is to consult with bishops of neighboring regions employing the same language.

Other conditions are also laid down, but the key points are contained here.

Another aspect of Article 36 which upholds the continued use of Latin has been pointed out by Professor Louis Salleron. Not only does Article 36 state specifically that Latin "is to be retained in the Latin rites" (in *ritibus latinis servetur*: the jussive subjunctive *servetur* denotes a command), but it can also be said to denote this in a negative manner. For had the three paragraphs which have been cited intended that the vernacular should become the norm, writes Professor Salleron, "the construction of the text would have been reversed. We would have read something like this: 'The use of vernacular languages will be introduced into the Latin rite . . .' and any exceptions or reservations in favor of the Latin language would then have been listed."[99]

This observation is reinforced by the instruction in Article 36.3 stating that the competent territorial authority can decide whether and to what extent the vernacular is to be used, in accordance with the norms laid down. The use of the word "whether" makes it quite clear that the vernacular need never be used at all. Similarly, Article 116 states:

The Church acknowledges Gregorian chant as proper to

---

99. Salleron, pp. 19-20.

the Roman liturgy: therefore, other things being equal, it should be given pride of place in liturgical services. Other kinds of sacred music, especially polyphony, are by no means excluded from liturgical celebrations, so long as they accord with the spirit of the liturgical action, as laid down in Article 30.

A good deal more could be written on this topic—but to little purpose. Perhaps Latin, Gregorian chant and polyphony have all but vanished from the generality of churches because they were considered obstacles to the active participation of the people, which the CSL had decreed should take priority over all else.

Results of the Liturgical Reforms

God forbid, warned Cardinal Heenan, that the *periti* should take control of the commissions established after the Council to interpret it to the world. But this is precisely what happened! The liberals had constructed the Constitution on the Sacred Liturgy as a weapon with which to initiate a revolution, and the Council Fathers had placed this weapon in the hands of the revolutionaries who had forged it. Archbishop R. J. Dwyer of Portland, Oregon observed, with the benefit of hindsight, that the great mistake of the Council Fathers was "to allow the implementation of the Constitution to fall into the hands of men who were either unscrupulous or incompetent. This is the so-called 'Liturgical Establishment,' a Sacred Cow which acts more like a White Elephant as it tramples the shards of a shattered liturgy with ponderous abandon."[100]

Cardinal Heenan was present in the Sistine Chapel for Father Bugnini's demonstration of his newly concocted experimental rite of Mass in 1967 (*Missa Normativa*), and he was dismayed by what he witnessed. He commented:

At home it is not only women and children but also fathers

---

100. *The Tidings*, July 9, 1971.

of families and young men who come regularly to Mass. If we were to offer them the kind of ceremony we saw yesterday in the Sistine Chapel we would soon be left with a congregation mostly of women and children.[101]

The Cardinal proved to be a true prophet. In 1976, a report on the state of Catholicism in the once flourishing archdiocese of Liverpool admitted that in many of its churches the congregations consisted mainly of primary school children, middle-aged, and elderly parishioners. "A vast number of young people between the ages of 15 and 25 have decided that Sunday Mass, as it is offered up in most parishes, has nothing to offer them."[102] Cardinal Heenan's prophecy was also confirmed in Article 69 of the working paper provided for the 1999 synod of European bishops in Rome. Commenting on the responses received from bishops in the pre-synodal survey, it stated:

> Certain responses mention somewhat problematic situations. In many countries of the West, liturgical celebrations are frequented almost exclusively by children and older people, especially women. The young and middle-aged are few in number. Such a situation runs the risk of projecting an image of a Church which is only for the elderly, women and children.

Comment is hardly necessary! Closed churches and plunging congregations are the undeniable fruit of the liturgical revolution. Detailed statistics illustrating the collapse in Mass attendance in the Western World are provided in Appendix II.

The traditional liturgy which formed the basis of popular piety was swept away in a mindless craze for novelty and ecumenical convergence. The capacity for destruction common to all revolutionaries is matched by no comparable tal-

---

101. This is an extract from the complete text of his intervention given to me by the Cardinal.
102. *The Tablet*, February 21, 1976.

ent for building, but this is something they refuse to admit. Their blindness has been well described by Professor James Hitchcock in one of the most perceptive books yet published on the collapse of Catholic faith and practice which followed the Council, a book which is all the more remarkable as it was published in 1972, only three years after the introduction of the Mass that was intended to regenerate a Church which, in fact, did not need regenerating:

> In general, radicals and many progressives regard the old liturgy much as they regard the old popular piety—disdainfully, as a collection of archaic, superstitious, and irrelevant practices in need of severe purification and restructuring by experts. Most liturgical reformers, however, if they ever understood the workings of the old liturgy, do not understand them now. They overlook the fact that this alleged religious desert attracted larger numbers of persons to voluntary daily observances than do the newer rites, a fact which can be explained only by assuming that pious laymen are mindless fools.[103]

The fact that even in 1966 the *Consilium* itself was still maintaining that permission for a vernacular Canon would never be granted to anyone indicates that the liturgical revolution had made an even more rapid conquest during and immediately after the Council than had been planned by the liturgical revolutionaries. One of France's best known radical liturgists has admitted: "Nothing in the Constitution on the Liturgy gave us any reason to suppose that, four or five years later, a single document would make it possible to bring in the Canon in modern languages."[104] Within ten years there were also eight additional "official Eucharistic Prayers" in modern languages. With the benefit of hindsight, recollecting the overwhelming vote of the bishops in favor of the Constitution on the Sacred Liturgy,

---

103. J. Hitchcock, *The Decline and Fall of Radical Catholicism* (New York: Doubleday, 1972), p. 178.

104. *Nouvelles Instructions pour la Réforme Liturgique* (Paris, 1967), pp. 12-13.

Archbishop R. J. Dwyer lamented:

> Who dreamed on that day that within a few years, far less
> than a decade, the Latin past of the Church would be all but
> expunged, that it would be reduced to a memory fading into
> the middle distance? The thought of it would have horrified
> us, but it seemed so far beyond the realm of the possible as
> to be ridiculous. So we laughed it off.[105]

A Pastoral Disaster

The effects of the reforms are now manifest for everyone
to see—and the most evident of these effects has been a
decline in Mass attendance, which has worsened in extent
the more radical the reforms have been. It fell from 41 per
cent of the population in France attending Mass in 1964 to
8 per cent in 2002—and where young people are concerned,
only 2% now assist at Mass.[106] It would certainly be impossible to prove that every Catholic who has ceased attending
Mass has done so because he dislikes the liturgical reforms.
Progressive liturgists claim that many Catholics do not go
because they would actually like the reforms to be more
radical! What any sociologist could certainly have pointed
out is that to disrupt completely the established customs of
any community in so drastic and abrupt a manner, particularly a community in which stability had always been so
important a characteristic, must certainly loosen the bonds
which hold its members together.

Pastorally, the reform has been a fiasco, a disaster. What
sort of success can be attributed to pastoral measures which
are followed by a large proportion of the flock—which they
are intended to help—leaving the sheepfold for new pas-
tures? All this has been done in the interests of a spurious

---

105. *Twin Circle*, October 26, 1973.
106. *La Croix*, December 24 and 25, 2002. The same report reveals the alarm-
    ing facts that while in 1962, 52% of priests in France were under 50 years
    of age, in 2000 it was only 11%. In 1960, 595 priests were ordained; in
    2000 the figure was 142.

form of ecumenism which has not brought true religious unity as much as one step nearer. "All these changes have but one justification," remarked Archbishop Lefebvre, "an aberrant senseless ecumenism that will not attract a single Protestant to the Faith, but will cause countless Catholics to lose it, and will instill total confusion into the minds of many more, who will no longer know what is true and what is false."[107] The complete accuracy of Archbishop Lefebvre's assessment of the nature and effects of the reform is made clear in an article written by a young and outspoken Italian prelate, Monsignor Domenico Celada. His remarks appeared in the Italian journal *lo Specchio* on May 16, 1969. Since that day the situation he described has worsened— year, after year, after year:

> The gradual destruction of the liturgy is a sad fact already well known. Within less than five years, the thousand year old structure of divine worship which throughout the centuries has been known as the *Opus Dei* has been dismantled. The beginning was the abolition of Latin, perpetrated in a fraudulent manner. The Council had in fact clearly laid down that "The use of the Latin language is to be preserved," while permitting the use of the vernacular in certain places, in certain cases, and in certain parts of the rite. By contrast, and in defiance of the authority of the Council, Latin has been suppressed practically everywhere, at all times, and in all parts of the rite. The Church's language has been abandoned, even at international liturgical functions. The universality of the Church is today claimed to be stressed by the use, on such occasions, of as many different languages as possible. The result is that—unless these are used simultaneously—all those parts of the rite which are not in one's own language become incomprehensible. It is Pentecost in reverse: while at Jerusalem the people *"ex omni natione, quae sub caelo est"* ["from every nation under heaven"] understood the words of the apostles, who were speaking but one language, so today, when all the different languages are spoken, nobody can understand anything. Instead of Pente-

---

107. *World Trends*, May 1974.

cost, we should rather speak of Babel. We have seen, during these past years, the abolition of those sublime gestures of devotion and piety, such as signs of the cross, kissing of the altar which symbolizes Christ, genuflections, etc., gestures which the secretary of the congregation responsible for liturgical reform, Father Annibale Bugnini, has dared publicly to describe as "anachronisms" and "wearisome externals." Instead, a puerile form of rite has been imposed, noisy, uncouth and extremely boring. And hypocritically, no notice has been taken of the disturbance and disgust of the faithful ... Resounding success has been claimed for it because a proportion of the faithful has been trained to repeat mechanically a succession of phrases which through repetition have already lost their effect. We have witnessed with horror the introduction into our churches of hideous parodies of the sacred texts, of tunes and instruments more suited to the tavern. And the instigator and persistent advocate of these so-called "youth masses" is none other than Father Annibale Bugnini. It is here recalled that he insisted on continuing the "yea, yca Masses" in Rome, and got his way despite the protest of Rome's Vicar General, Cardinal Dell'Acqua. During the pontificate of John XXIII, Bugnini had been expelled from the Lateran University where he was a teacher of liturgy precisely because he held such ideas—only to become, later, secretary of the congregation dealing with liturgical reform.

Mass and Sacraments Reformed by a Freemason?

It would be impossible to place too much stress upon the fact that Archbishop Bugnini was the moving spirit behind the entire liturgical reform—a point which, with surprising lack of discretion, *l'Osservatore Romano* emphasized when it attempted to camouflage the reason for his abrupt dismissal by lavishing praise upon him. Archbishop Bugnini was, the Vatican journal explained, the co-ordinator and animator who had directed the work of the commissions.[108]

---

108. *l'Osservatore Romano*, July 20, 1975.

It also needs to be stressed that the liturgical reform was not concerned solely with the Mass, but extended to all the Sacraments, not hesitating to interfere in some instances with their very matter and form. The wholesale and drastic nature of this reform constitutes a breach with Tradition unprecedented in the history of the Church—and the fact that the co-ordinator and animator who directed it was removed from his position because Pope Paul VI believed him to be a Freemason must rightly give every faithful Catholic cause for alarm. This book has been concerned primarily with the Mass, but the changes made in some of the other sacramental rites give equal cause for concern. The modifications made in the Rite of Ordination are, if anything, even more serious than those made in the Mass.[109] Pope Paul himself had to intervene and personally correct the very serious deficiencies in the new Order of Baptism for Infants, which had been promulgated with his approval in 1969.[110] This provides another demonstration of the fact that papally approved liturgical texts are not, and should not be, exempt from criticism—particularly when they involve changes in traditional rites. Had the Pope not been made aware of the serious disquiet aroused by the new Order of Baptism for Infants, he might not have re-examined it and made the important revisions which he promulgated in 1973.

Finally, some comfort at least can be taken from the fact that Archbishop Bugnini's alleged Masonic associations were discovered in time to prevent his fully implementing the fourth and final stage of his revolution. He had divided this revolution into four stages—firstly, the transition from Latin to the vernacular; secondly, the reform of the liturgical books; thirdly, the translation of the liturgical books; and fourthly, as he explained in his journal *Notitiae*, "the adaptation or 'incarnation' of the Roman form of the liturgy into the usages and mentalities of each individual Church is

---

109. Cf. M. Davies, *The Order of Melchisedech* (Harrison, NY: Roman Catholic Books, 1993).
110. *Notitiae*, No. 85, July-August, 1973, pp. 268-272.

now beginning and will be pursued with ever increasing care and preparation."[111] Archbishop Bugnini made this boast in 1974, and in some countries, India in particular, the fourth stage was already well advanced when he was removed from his position in 1975. Only time will reveal whether it has been possible to contain or even reverse this process of adaptation—and the extent to which the desire to reverse it exists in the Vatican.

The Roman Rite Has Been Destroyed

Father Louis Bouyer, devastated by the contrast between what, as a leading member of the Liturgical Movement, he had hoped the implementation of the CSL would achieve, and what it did in fact achieve, had the integrity to state:

> We must speak plainly: there is practically no liturgy worthy of the name today in the Catholic Church.[112]

Msgr. Gamber sums up the true effect of the post-conciliar reform in one devastating sentence:

> At this critical juncture, the traditional Roman rite, more than one thousand years old, has been destroyed.[113]

Is he exaggerating? Not at all. His claim is endorsed from the opposite end of the liturgical spectrum by that "great master of the international liturgical world," Father Joseph Gelineau, who remarks with commendable honesty and no sign of regret:

> Let those who like myself have known and sung a Latin-Gregorian High Mass remember it if they can. Let them compare it with the Mass that we now have. Not only the words, the melodies, and some of the gestures are different.

---

111. *Notitiae*, No. 92, April 1974, p. 126.
112. Bouyer, p. 99.
113. Gamber, p. 99.

To tell the truth, it is a different liturgy of the Mass. This needs to be said without ambiguity: the Roman Rite as we knew it no longer exists (*le rite romain tel que nous l'avons connu n'existe plus*). It has been destroyed (*il est détruit*).[114]

The CSL has already been cited to the effect that "This most sacred Council declares that holy Church holds all lawfully acknowledged rites to be of equal authority and dignity: that she wishes to preserve them in the future and to foster them in every way." How you preserve and foster something by destroying it is something that even Archbishop Bugnini might have found difficult to explain. The Archbishop, of course, insisted that he was responsible not for destruction, but for restoration, and that from 1948 he had spent "twenty-seven years devoted to restoring splendor and charm, youthful beauty, trenchancy, and a sweet fragrance to the public prayer of the Church."[115] Those who remember the liturgy as it was, or have the good fortune to assist at the Traditional Mass today, will beg to differ with Archbishop Bugnini and will concur with Msgr. Gamber:

> The real destruction of the traditional Mass, of the traditional Roman rite with a history of more than one thousand years, is the wholesale destruction of the Faith on which it was based, a Faith that had been the source of our piety and of our courage to bear witness to Christ and His Church, the inspiration of countless Catholics over many centuries. Will someone, some day, be able to say the same thing about the new Mass?[116]

They certainly will not! The total incompatibility of any radical reform of the Catholic liturgy with the ethos and traditions of the Church is well expressed by Professor James Hitchcock:

---

114. Gelineau, pp. 9-10.
115. Bugnini, p. xxiii.
116. Gamber, p. 102.

The radical and deliberate alteration of ritual leads inevitably to the radical alteration of belief as well. This radical alteration causes an immediate loss of contact with the living past of the community, which comes instead to be a deadening burden. The desire to shed the burden of the past is incompatible with Catholicism, which accepts history as an organic development from ancient roots and expresses this acceptance in a deep respect for Tradition.[117]

Loss of Faith

The most evident instance of the fact that the radical alteration of ritual leads to the radical alteration of belief is, of course, the reform of the apostate Thomas Cranmer. In his classic history of the Reformation in England, Monsignor Philip Hughes explains:

> All but insensibly, as the years went by, the beliefs enshrined in the old, and now disused, rites, and kept alive by these rites in men's minds and affections, would disappear—without the need of any systematic missionary effort to preach them down.[118]

Thus, in the reign of Elizabeth I (1558-1603), the majority of English Catholics, and almost all their children, lost their faith in the Real Presence, not by a preaching campaign against it, but by participating for decades in a liturgy from which the ritual signs of reverence, which kept this belief alive in their minds and affections, had been removed. That the radical and deliberate alteration of the ritual of the Mass since Vatican II has led inevitably to the radical alteration of belief in the Real Presence was made clear in the February 1995 issue of *Homiletic and Pastoral Review*. An article by Germain Grisez and Russell Shaw lamented the fact that

---

117. James Hitchcock, *The Recovery of the Sacred* (New York: Seabury Press, 1974), p. 59
118. Philip Hughes, *The Reformation in England*, vol. II (London: Hollis & Carter, 1953), p. 111.

belief in the Real Presence in the United States "has not simply grown dim, but, seemingly, been extinguished." The two authors blamed some of the authorized or mandated changes in the liturgy since the Second Vatican Council, such as the use of English in the Eucharistic Prayer, the multiplication of the forms of that prayer, the emphasis on the celebrating community, the reduction of the Eucharistic fast, Communion in the hand, and the exchange of the sign of peace before Communion. The conclusion of Grisez and Shaw is that "In the general crisis of the Church in the USA, no individual crisis is more serious and urgent than this one."[119] The survey on which they based this judgment showed that most American Catholics today describe the consecrated bread and wine at Mass as "symbolic reminders" of Christ rather than things that are changed into the Body and Blood of Christ. Only among Catholics 65 and older did even the slimmest majority—51 percent—say that at Mass the bread and wine are changed into Christ's Body and Blood, instead of serving merely as symbolic reminders of Christ. Among Catholics in the age-brackets 18-29 and 30-44, 70 percent considered the consecrated Host and Precious Blood to be merely "symbolic reminders."

During the 45-year reign of Elizabeth I, belief in the Real Presence among English Catholics was transformed into belief in the real absence. This is already becoming the case in the English-speaking world within four decades of what a Monsignor friend of mine calls the Second Vatican Disaster.

---

119. In the Traditional Latin Mass, only the consecrated hands of a priest could touch the sacred vessels or the Host. Laymen received Holy Communion kneeling, on the tongue, and only from the consecrated hands of a priest. In a typical parish today, Holy Communion is received in the hand, from an extraordinary minister (lay person), by a standing communicant. This means that every traditional sign of reverence has been abandoned or made optional, and belief in the Real Presence has been abandoned with these signs of reverence. The innovators have, as Dietrich von Hildebrand expressed it, replaced holy intimacy with Christ by an unbecoming familiarity, discouraged reverence in the face of mystery, precluded awe, and all but extinguished a sense of sacredness. (Cf. p. 40 above.)

The Mass That Will Not Die

The beauty, the worth, the perfection of the Traditional Latin Mass of the Catholic Church, so universally acknowledged and admired, was described by Fr. Faber in his book *The Blessed Sacrament* as "the most beautiful thing this side of Heaven." He continues:

> It came forth out of the grand mind of the Church, and lifted us out of earth and out of self, and wrapped us round in a cloud of mystical sweetness and the sublimities of a more than angelic liturgy, and purified us almost without ourselves, and charmed us with celestial charming, so that our very senses seem to find vision, hearing, fragrance, taste and touch beyond what earth can give.[120]

Archbishop Bugnini intended to consign this angelic liturgy to oblivion. However, this rite of Mass, which Cardinal Newman said that he could attend forever and not be tired, has proved to be *the Mass that will not die*. It is celebrated more often with every day that passes, and all those who have a true *sensus catholicus*, a Catholic instinct, will concur with Msgr. Gamber:

> In the final analysis, this means that in the future the traditional rite of Mass must be retained in the Roman Catholic Church . . . as the primary liturgical form for the celebration of Mass. It must become once more the norm of our faith and the symbol of Catholic unity throughout the world, a rock of stability in a period of upheaval and never-ending change.[121]

---

120. Cited in N. Gihr, *The Holy Sacrifice of the Mass* (St. Louis, MO: B. Herder, 1908), p. 337.
121. Gamber, p. 114.

Appendix I

The Participation of Protestant Observers
In the Compilation of
The New Catholic Liturgical Rites

On May 3, 1970, *La Documentation Catholique* published the text of a speech made by Pope Paul VI to the members of the *Consilium*. The cover of this issue depicted Pope Paul VI posing with the six Protestant Observers who had been invited to participate in the work of the *Consilium*. This photograph proved to be a source of astonishment and even scandal to large numbers of the faithful, who had no idea that Protestants had played any part in the compilation of the new Catholic sacramental rites. It resulted in public controversy in a number of countries, which was followed by official denials that the Observers had in fact played any part in the compilation of the new rites. These denials have since been cited by apologists for the official reform as "refutations" of the allegation that Protestant Observers had taken an active part in their compilation. There is, however, a considerable difference between a denial and a refutation, and these particular denials are totally gratuitous and contradict the available evidence.

In the July-August 1974 issue of *Notitiae*, official journal of the Sacred Congregation for Divine Worship, Archbishop Bugnini (its Secretary) claimed that the Observers confined their role simply to observing (pp. 249-250). Here are his exact words:

> What role did the "Observers" play in the Consilium?
> Nothing more than that of —"Observers." First of all, they

only took part in the study meetings. In the second place, they behaved with impeccable discretion. They never intervened in the discussions and never asked to speak.

On February 25, 1976, the Director of the Vatican Press Office gave the following reply to a question by the journalist Georges Huber as to whether the Protestant Observers had participated in the elaboration of the New Mass: "The Protestant Observers did not participate in the elaboration of the texts of the new Missal." This denial was printed in *La Documentation Catholique* on July 4, 1976.

In contrast with this, Bishop W. W. Baum (now Cardinal Baum), an ardent ecumenist, made the following statement in a personal interview with *The Detroit News*, June 27, 1967:

> They are not simply there as observers, *but as consultants as well*, and they *participate fully* in the discussions on Catholic liturgical renewal. It wouldn't mean much if they just listened, but they contributed. (Emphasis added.)

In order to place this statement in its correct context it must be made clear that, at the time he made it, Bishop Baum was executive director of the American Catholic Bishops' Commission on Ecumenical Affairs and the first Catholic spokesman ever invited to address the General Synod of the United Church of Christ, an American Protestant denomination. During his address, he revealed to the delegates that Protestant scholars "have had a voice" in the revision of the Catholic liturgy. As a follow-up to this revelation, Harold Acharhern, religious correspondent of the *Detroit News*, obtained the interview with Bishop Baum from which I have quoted.

The account given by Cardinal Baum, and the denials issued by Archbishop Bugnini and the Vatican Press Office, are clearly contradictory. In order to discover the truth, I wrote to one of the Observers, Canon Ronald Jasper. Before giving his reply, it is necessary to explain the manner in which the *Consilium* did its work. Firstly, there were the study sessions, during which the practical details of the reform were worked out, discussed and modified. Then there were the formal (plenary) meetings during which the draft services which had been compiled in the study sessions were debated and voted upon. In my letter to Canon Jasper, I explained that I was working upon a series of books on the liturgical reform and that I particularly wished to know whether the Observers had had a voice in the new rites of Mass and Ordination. In his reply, dated February 10, 1977, he explained that the Observers received all the documents from the drafters of the new services in the same way as did other members of the *Consilium*. They were then present at the debates when the new services were presented by the experts and debated by the *Consilium*, but the Observers were not allowed to join in the debate.

In the afternoon, however, they always had an informal meeting with the *periti* who had prepared the draft services, and at these meetings they were certainly allowed to comment and criticize and make suggestions. It was then for the *periti* to decide whether any of their points were worth taking up when the general debates in the *Consilium* were resumed. But, explained Canon Jasper, in conclusion, these informal meetings were a complete free-for-all, and there was a very frank exchange of views.

Exactly the same process took place during the course of Vatican II. The Protestant Observers, while not allowed to speak in the plenary sessions, were able to take an active part in the informal discussions where the real work of drafting the documents was done. Their influence is visible in the finalized documents themselves, and evidence of it is provided in Chapter IX of *Pope John's Council*. In addition to this evidence, the following testimonies are relevant.

Archdeacon Pawley, an Anglican Observer, reveals that "In the course of the Council itself the fullest courtesies and opportunities for communication and exchange were allowed to the Observers at every stage, and traces of the process can be recognized in the documents themselves."[1]

Robert McAfee Brown, a Presbyterian Observer, remarks:

> Particularly during the discussion on ecumenism, it was apparent that many bishops wanted to know what Protestant reactions were to statements in the *schema* about Protestantism, and wanted to elicit Protestant opinions on how the *schema* could be improved. Thus, although we had no direct "voice" on the Council floor, we did indeed have an indirect voice through the many contacts that were possible with the Fathers and their indispensable strong right arms, the *periti*.[2]

Dr. R. McAfee Brown also reveals that there were occasions when the Observers were able to have a direct voice on the floor. "Is there anything you Observers want said on the Council floor about *De Oecumenismo?*" one bishop asked.[3] The Observers then put their views in writing, to be incorporated into written interventions made on their behalf by bishops.

Thus, although it could be argued that officially the Observers played no part in drafting the conciliar documents, as they could neither vote nor speak in the debates, it is clear that they were able to influence the final format of these documents. This is precisely what took place with the formulation of the new liturgical rites by the post-conciliar *Consilium*.

---

1. B. Pawley, *Rome and Canterbury through Four Centuries* (London: Mowbray, 1974), p. 343.
2. R. McAfee Brown, *Observer in Rome* (London: Methuen, 1964), pp. 227-228.
3. *Ibid.*, p. 173.

Appendix II

The Fruits of the Liturgical Reforms

Both the Holy See and national hierarchies deny emphatically that a disastrous liturgical revolution has taken place in the Catholic Church, especially in the liturgy, since the Second Vatican Council, and they insist that the Catholic faithful are the fortunate beneficiaries of a fruitful renewal. This official viewpoint was expressed by Pope John Paul II in his Apostolic Letter *Vicesimus Quintus Annus* of December 4, 1988, commemorating the twenty-fifth anniversary of the Second Vatican Council's Constitution on the Sacred Liturgy. The Pope explained, quoting the Constitution itself, that the objectives of the reform were "To impart an ever increasing vigor to the Christian life of the faithful; to adapt more suitably to the needs of our own times those institutions that are subject to change; to foster whatever can promote union among all who believe in Christ; to strengthen whatever can help to call the whole of humanity into the household of the Church." (Par. 1). The Pope continued, "The vast majority of the pastors and the Christian people have accepted the liturgical reform in a spirit of obedience and indeed joyful fervor. For this we should give thanks to God for that movement of the Holy Spirit in the Church which the liturgical renewal represents. . . ." (Par. 12).

In his sermon for Pentecost 2001, Pope John Paul II rendered homage to John XXIII on the occasion of the 38th anniversary of his death:[1]

---

1. It was on this occasion that the mortal remains of the deceased Pope were exposed in St. Peter's square and, after the ceremony, were escorted in procession before the Altar of the Confession in the Vatican basilica to be exposed for the veneration of the faithful.

The Second Vatican Council, announced, convoked, and opened by Pope John XXIII, was conscious of this vocation of the Church. One can well say that the Holy Spirit was the protagonist of the Council from the moment the Pope convoked it, declaring that he had welcomed as coming from above an interior voice that imposed itself upon his spirit. This "gentle breeze" became a "violent wind" and the conciliar event took the form of a new Pentecost. "It is, indeed, in the doctrine and spirit of Pentecost," affirmed Pope John, "that the great event which is an ecumenical council draws its substance and its life." (*Discorsi*, p. 398).[2]

On March 5, 2000, *The Catholic Times* (London) reported the Pope as stating that the little seed planted by Pope John XXIII has become "a tree which has spread its majestic and mighty branches over the vineyard of the Lord." He added that "It has given us many fruits in these 35 years of life, and it will give us many more in the years to come."

With all the respect that is due to the Holy Father, the fact that there has been no renewal cannot be changed simply because he would like a renewal to have taken place.[3] If the fruits of the Vatican II liturgical reform are to be compared to a tree, Matthew Chapter 7, verses 16-19, comes to mind immediately: *A fructibus eorum cognoscetis eos*—"By

---

2. *Documentation Catholique*, July 1, 2001, No. 2251.
3. A Catholic is in no way disloyal to the Church if he feels bound to disagree with the Pope on a question of fact. Many devout Catholics tend to accept every statement by a pope as if it were an infallible pronouncement. That this is not the case was made clear by Cardinal Newman in his book *Certain Difficulties Felt by Anglicans in Catholic Teaching*. (London: Pickering, 1876, p. 325). Newman explains: "He speaks *ex cathedra*, or infallibly, when he speaks, first, as the Universal Teacher; secondly, in the name and with the authority of the Apostles; thirdly, on a point of faith or morals; fourthly, with the purpose of binding every member of the Church to accept and believe his decision. These conditions of course contract the range of his infallibility most materially. Hence Billuart speaking of the Pope says, 'Neither in conversation, nor in discussion, nor in interpreting Scripture or the Fathers, nor in consulting, nor in giving his reasons for the point which he has defined, nor in answering letters, nor in private deliberations, supposing he is setting forth his own opinion, is the Pope infallible.'"

their fruits you shall know them. Do men gather grapes of thorns, or figs of thistles? Even so, every good tree bringeth forth good fruit, and the evil tree bringeth forth evil fruit. A good tree cannot bring forth evil fruit, neither can an evil tree bring forth good fruit."

In his Encyclical Letter *Ecclesia de Eucharistia* of April 17, 2003, Pope John Paul II once more insisted that the Vatican II liturgical reform has been followed by a renewal rather than a revolution, by good fruits rather than bad fruits:

> The Magisterium's commitment to proclaiming the Eucharistic mystery has been matched by interior growth within the Christian community. Certainly *the liturgical reform inaugurated by the Council* has greatly contributed to a more conscious, active and fruitful participation in the Holy Sacrifice of the Altar on the part of the faithful. In many places, adoration of the Blessed Sacrament is also an important daily practice and becomes an inexhaustible source of holiness. The devout participation of the faithful in the Eucharistic procession on the Solemnity of the Body and Blood of Christ is a grace from the Lord which yearly brings joy to those who take part in it. Other positive signs of Eucharistic faith and love might also be mentioned. (*Emphasis added*).

Once again, with all due respect to the Holy Father, one must insist that if there has indeed been an "interior growth within the Christian community," it is certainly not reflected in the catastrophic collapse of Catholic life in First World countries, which is documented beyond any possible doubt in the statistics which follow. While the inauguration of perpetual adoration in some parishes and chapels in recent years is an admirable development, one must look at the overall state of the Church: in fact, as Germain Grisez and Russel Shaw made clear above, belief in the Real Presence in the United States "has not simply grown dim, but, seemingly, been extinguished." In the September 3, 1999 edition of the British *Catholic Herald*, it was reported that shortly before his death Cardinal Basil Hume of Westminster had lamented the fact that Catholics in England had lost devotion to the Eucharist, which lies at the heart of the Catholic Faith. He blamed the lack of Eucharistic devotion on "the way children are taught the faith by adults." This is an astonishing claim in view of the fact that, like his fellow bishops, he had imposed textbooks in which the traditional teaching was ignored.

Then, in what seems to be a *volte face*, the Holy Father admits that, in some places at least, Eucharistic discipline and even faith are suffering very serious problems, and he provides a list of the liturgical deviations and abuses concerning which traditional Catholics have been protesting since the first changes were imposed upon the faithful. These abuses take place, the Holy Father tells us, alongside the lights to which he has referred, but he nowhere tells us where these lights are shining:

> Unfortunately, alongside these lights, *there are also shadows*. In some places the practice of Eucharistic adoration has been almost completely abandoned. In various parts of the Church, abuses have occurred, leading to confusion with regard to sound faith and Catholic doctrine concerning this wonderful sacrament. At times one encounters an extremely reductive understanding of the Eucharistic mystery. Stripped of its sacrificial meaning, it is celebrated as if it were simply a fraternal banquet. Furthermore, the necessity of the ministerial priesthood, grounded in apostolic succession, is at times obscured, and the sacramental nature of the Eucharist is reduced to its mere effectiveness as a form of proclamation. This has led here and there to ecumenical initiatives which, albeit well-intentioned, indulge in Eucharistic practices contrary to the discipline by which the Church expresses her faith. How can we not express profound grief at all this? The Eucharist is too great a gift to tolerate ambiguity and depreciation. It is my hope that the present Encyclical Letter will effectively help to banish the dark clouds of unacceptable doctrine and practice, so that the Eucharist will continue to shine forth in all its radiant mystery. (*Emphasis added.*)

These deplorable abuses did not exist before the Vatican II liturgical reform, and it can hardly be denied that they are indeed the true fruits of the reform. We must indeed pray that this encyclical, which contains much admirable Eucharistic teaching, will help "to banish the dark clouds of unacceptable doctrine and practice," but alas, these have now become so ingrained in parish life that, short of a miracle, they will not be eradicated. The well-entrenched liturgical bureaucracy throughout the First World completely ignores admonitions from Rome which conflict with their agenda. They treat the Vatican and the Pope himself with what can be described accurately as amused contempt. In November 1997 the Vatican published a document entitled *Instruction on Certain Questions concerning the Collaboration of the Lay Faithful in the Ministry of Priests*. It was intended to curb such abuses as the infestation of Catholic sanctuaries by a plague of unnecessary extraordinary ministers of Holy Communion. *Catholic World Report* of February 1998 carried a scathing editorial entitled "One More Document," with the sub-title "If Church discipline is never enforced, how much do formal statements matter?" The editorial commented on the response to the Instruction:

> As we survey the Catholic scene we see no change whatsoever. In the parishes where those abuses occurred last year, they are still occurring today . . . These and other liturgical abuses have been condemned again. The condemnations have no practical effect . . .In an ordinary household when children misbehave, does the father issue a statement of policy—and then when they ignore his words, another new statement in response to each repeated transgression . . . There is a time for action.

As was shown above, the action that follows defiance of a command from Rome to correct an abuse tends to be to legalize the abuse; the abject surrender on the question of altar girls is an evident example. The fact that some practices which began as abuses have now become the norm was admitted by the Congregation for Divine Worship in its journal *Notitiae* as long ago as 1992. In an editorial entitled "The Credibility of the Liturgical Reform" (*Credibilità della Riforma Liturgica*), which went virtually unreported, it admitted that "the credibility of the liturgical reform is being put in jeopardy after thirty years of non-homogeneous application" (*la credibilità della riforma liturgica venga posta in pericolo . . .*) and that:

> The malformations born in the first years of the application still endure, and gradually, as new generations follow one another, could almost become the rule (*esse potrebbero diventare quasi una regola*). Thus, the letter and the spirit of the liturgical reform remain in some cases in the shadows, and customs are created which certainly originated after the liturgical reform, but not in its genuine sense, and with consequences more negative for liturgical formation than those customs connected to praxes before Vatican II.[4]

Highly significant is the admission by the Congregation that these abuses did not exist before the Council.

Cardinal Paul Poupard, President of the Pontifical Council for Culture, stated bluntly in January 2000: "The dechristianization of Europe is a reality."[5] This is hardly an indication of "interior growth within the Christian community." Cardinal Daneels of Brussels, Belgium, stated in an interview with the London *Catholic Times* on May 12, 2000 that the Church in Europe is facing extinction. He lamented the vocations crisis in the West and remarked that "Without priests the sacramental life of the Church will disappear. We will become a Protestant Church without sacraments. We will be another type of Church, not Catholic."[6] During the Synod of European Bishops in October 1999, Archbishop Fernando Sebastián Aguilar of Pamplona gave the

---

4. *Notitiae*, 315, vol. 28 (1992), pp. 625-628.
5. *Le Spectacle du Monde*, January 2000.
6. *Catholic Times*, May 12, 2000.

following gloomy but realistic assessment of Spanish Catholicism:

> For 40 or 50 years, Spanish society has moved far away from the Church and the explicit acknowledgement of the treasures of the Kingdom of God. Cultural and spiritual secularization has affected many members of the Church. The result of this has been the weakening of the faith and divine revelation, the theoretical and practical questioning of Christian moral teaching, the massive abandonment of attending Sunday Mass, the non-acceptance of the Magisterium of the Church in those points that do not coincide with the trends of the dominant culture. The cultural convictions on which social life is based are undermined and are more atheistic than Christian.

The situation in Spain is parallelled throughout Europe and the entire First World, not least in English-speaking countries. This is particularly true where the teaching given in Catholic educational institutions at every level is concerned. The catechetical bureaucracies set up by the hierarchies threw out the traditional catechism and replaced it with an endless series of new texts. Having taught in a Catholic school throughout the thirty years following the Council, I can testify that these texts soon reached the point where they could hardly be termed even vestigially Catholic. New methods of teaching the Catholic religion were replaced by a requirement to teach a new religion that was not Catholic. Parents, priests and teachers who protested were treated as Neanderthals. Countless protests were made to Rome, but they were ignored. Vatican policy has been to uphold the authority of the diocesan bishop, even if he is using that authority to destroy the Faith. In 1977 a very good friend of mine, the late Canon George Telford, resigned from his position as Vice Chairman of the department of Catechetics for England and Wales because, he assured me, there was not even one bishop in the country who was even interested in ensuring that children in Catholic schools were taught the Catholic Faith. In his letter of resignation he stated bluntly: "Modern catechetics is theologically corrupt and spiritually bankrupt. Its structures and innovations are irrelevant and unmeaningful for the Catholic Faith, and can achieve nothing but its gradual dilution."[7]

The Australian Catholic monthly, *AD 2000*, in its January 2003 issue, reported a speech made by Professor Denis McLaughlin of the Australian Catholic University (ACU) to the national conference of Australian secondary school principals in October 2002. His audience would certainly not have been pleased with what he had to say. His speech reported the findings of a survey that he had conducted into the beliefs, values and practices of Catholic student teachers. The survey found that most student teachers did not accept the Church's teaching in such areas as the Eucharist, abortion, contraception and women's ordination, and there were no significant differences between the views of first year and final year students. This kind of thinking, according to Professor McLaughlin, is also to be found among practicing Catholic school teachers, indicating that the downward spiral of belief and practice in the general Catholic population shows no sign of leveling out:

> The cult of individualism and subjectivism, so prevalent in modern Western culture, has also had its impact on religious education. This has led to the present widespread ignorance of the basics of the Faith and their intellectual and historical underpinnings, making an already difficult situation for any religious faith commitment close to impossible. It is no wonder so many Catholics have made their peace with secularism and materialism under a thin veneer of cultural Catholicity. Their views on "gay" rights, divorce, abortion or women priests are indistinguishable from those of the rest of the population.

The professor's own ACU research confirms findings from

---

7. *Christian Order*, April 1977, p. 205.

other sources, such as the Catholic Church Life Survey and Brother Marcellin Flynn:

> Data obtained by ACU researchers in Sydney found that 97 per cent of young Catholics abandoned the practice of their faith within 12 months of completing high school . . . In other words, despite up to 13 years of religious education, most young Catholics reject the very foundations of the Faith.

The descriptions by Canon Telford and Professor McLaughlin of the abysmal state of religious teaching in Britain and Australia are equally applicable to the United States. The stage has been reached where, if parents wish their children to know the Faith, they must teach it to them themselves, a task which, in fact, is their primary duty. In doing so, it is imperative that they themselves be completely sure of the doctrines that they teach, and a great service for concerned parents was provided by TAN Books and Publishers, Inc. when it reissued what is probably the best compendium of the Faith on a popular level available in English: *This Is The Faith* by Canon Francis Ripley, who had worked very closely with Canon Telford in his unsuccessful campaign to have the Catholic Faith taught in Catholic schools. This book was widely used in inquiry classes and should be familiar to every Catholic adult.[8]

Statistics relating to England and Wales and the United States are appended to demonstrate that what we are witnessing is not a new Pentecost but a disastrous and apparently terminal decline. These statistics are paralleled in every country of what is known as the First World. It is true that there has been an increase in the overall number of seminarians and ordinations since Vatican II, but this increase has taken place primarily in Third World areas, such as Africa and Asia and, when examined carefully,

---

8. Fr. Francis Ripley, *This Is The Faith* (Rockford, IL: TAN edition, 1951/2002).

cannot be attributed to the influence of the Council, but to sociological factors, which will not be examined in this appendix, which is concerned only with the First World. I will give just one example derived from a visit to an Indian seminary in 1988. The seminary was completely full and could have been filled four times over; but in India, Ordination gives a man a certain social status and a guaranteed income, coming largely from abroad, which enables him to give financial support to his family. The doctrinal formation given in the seminary was of very dubious orthodoxy. I asked the rector, who wore no priestly attire, if the seminarians studied St. Thomas Aquinas, and he burst out laughing. The walls of his office were decorated with pictures of scantily clad American female country singers. I asked the reason, and the rector replied that it enabled the seminarians to relate to him.

The Incredible Shrinking Church
In England and Wales

The most evident characteristic of the Catholic Church in England and Wales is that it is shrinking at an incredible rate into what must be termed a state of terminal decline. The official *Catholic Directory* documents a steady increase in every important aspect of Catholic life until the mid-sixties: then the decline sets in. The figures for marriages and baptisms are not simply alarming, but disastrous. In 1944 there were 30,946 marriages, by 1964 the figure had risen to 45,592—but by 1999 it had plunged to 13,814, well under half the figure for 1944. The figures for baptisms for the same years are 71,604 (1944), 137,673 (1964), and 63,158 (1999). With fewer children born to Catholic couples each year, the number of marriages must inevitably continue to decline, with even fewer children born—and so on. Nor can it be presumed that even half the children who are baptized will be practicing their Faith by the time they reach their teens. An examination of the figures for a typical diocese indicates that less than half the children who are baptized are confirmed, and a report in *The Universe* as long ago as 1990 gave an estimate of only 11% of young Catholics practicing their Faith when they leave high school.

Apart from marriages and baptisms, Mass attendance is the most accurate guide to the vitality of the Catholic community. The figure has plunged from 2,114,219 in 1966 to 1,041,728 in 1999 and is still falling at a rate of about 32,000 a year.

In 1944, 178 priests were ordained; in 1964, 230; and in 1999 only 43—and in the same year 121 priests died.

In 1985, twenty years after the Second Vatican Council, bishops from all over the world assembled in Rome to assess the impact of the Council. This gave them the opportunity to admit that their implementation of it had been disastrous, and that drastic measures must be taken to give the Faith a viable future in First World countries.

Cardinal Basil Hume of Westminster insisted, on behalf of the bishops of England and Wales, that there must be no turning back from the policies they had adopted to implement the Council. A report in *The Universe* of December 13, 1985 informed us that the Synod had adopted Cardinal Hume's position without a single dissenting voice. The final sentence of this report must be described as ironically prophetic: "In the meantime the people of God have a firm mandate to further Exodus along the route mapped out by the Second Vatican Council." Change the upper case "E" of Exodus to a lower case "e," exodus, and this is precisely what has happened—and the exodus will continue until Catholicism in England and Wales vanishes into oblivion within thirty years, if not sooner. Without a divine intervention, the "Second Spring" of the Catholic Faith in England predicted by Cardinal Newman (1801-1890) will end in the bleakest of winters.

The Incredible Shrinking Church
In the United States

In March 2003 there was published in St. Louis what is

certainly the most important statistical survey of the Church in the United States since Vatican II: *Index of Leading Catholic Indicators: The Church Since Vatican II*, by Kenneth C. Jones.[9] It provides meticulously documented statistics on every aspect of Catholic life subject to statistical verification, and it is illustrated with graphs which depict in a dramatic visual manner the catastrophic collapse of Catholic life in the United States since the Council. With the publication of this book, no rational person could disagree with Father Louis Bouyer that, "Unless we are blind, we must even state bluntly that what we see looks less like the hoped-for regeneration of Catholicism than its accelerated decomposition."[10]

Mr. Jones has given me his permission to quote from the introduction to his book, but before doing so, I must quote from a news story in the March 23, 2003 issue of the London *Universe*. Under the headline *"En Suite Monastery,"* it reports: "A former Irish Carmelite monastery is expected to be turned into a country-club style hotel after its sale to a property developer. The Carmelite order had shut their house in Castle Martyr, Cork, last year after 73 years because of the downfall in vocations." This is but one of thousands of similar examples of the actual, as opposed to the fantasy, fruits of Vatican II. On page 100 of Mr. Jones' book there is a graph revealing that the number of Carmelite seminarians in the United States has decreased from 545 in 1965 to 46 in 2000—a decline of 92 percent. This figure seems positively healthy when compared with the graph on page 99, relating to the La Salette Fathers, which reveals a decline in the number of seminarians for the same period from 552 to just 1. Figures and graphs for every major religious order are set out in the book, and it

---

9. K. Jones, *Index of Leading Catholic Indicators*. Mailing address of Kenneth Jones: 11939 Manchester Rd., #217, St. Louis, MO 63131. www.catholicindicators.com
10. L. Bouyer, *The Decomposition of Catholicism* (Chicago: Franciscan Herald Press, 1970), p. 1.

would be hard to disagree with Mr. Jones that "The religious orders will soon be virtually non-existent in the United States." In the introduction to his book he writes:

When Pope John XXIII opened the Second Vatican Council in 1962, the Catholic Church in America was in the midst of an unprecedented period of growth. Bishops were ordaining record numbers of priests and building scores of seminaries to handle the surge in vocations. Young women by the thousands gave up lives of comfort for the austerity of the convent. These nuns taught millions of students in the huge system of parochial and private schools.

The ranks of Catholics swelled as parents brought in their babies for Baptism and adult converts flocked to the Church. Lines outside the confessionals were long, and by some estimates three quarters of the faithful went to Mass every Sunday. Given this favorable state of affairs, some Catholics wondered at the time whether an ecumenical council was opportune — don't rock the boat, they said.

The Holy Father chided these people in his opening speech to the Council: "We feel we must disagree with those prophets of gloom who are always forecasting disaster, as though the end of the world were at hand." Forty years later the end has not arrived. But we are now facing the disaster.

Even some in the Vatican have recognized it. Cardinal Joseph Ratzinger, Prefect of the Congregation for the Doctrine of the Faith, said: "Certainly the results [of Vatican II] seem cruelly opposed to the expectations of everyone, beginning with those of Pope John XXIII and then of Pope Paul VI . . ."

Since Cardinal Ratzinger made these remarks in 1984, the crisis in the Church has accelerated. In every area that is statistically verifiable—for example, the number of priests, seminarians, priestless parishes, nuns, Mass attendance, converts and annulments—the "process of decadence" is apparent.

I have gathered these statistics in the *Index of Leading Catholic Indicators* because the magnitude of the emergency is unknown to many. Beyond a vague understanding of a "vocations crisis," both the faithful and the general public have no idea how bad things have been since the close of the

Second Vatican Council in 1965. Here are some of the stark facts:

• **Priests**. After skyrocketing from about 27,000 in 1930 to 58,000 in 1965, the number of priests in the United States dropped to 45,000 in 2002. By 2020,[11] there will be about 31,000 priests—and only 15,000 will be under the age of 70. Right now there are more priests aged 80 to 84 than there are aged 30 to 34.

• **Ordinations**. In 1965 there were 1,575 ordinations to the priesthood, in 2002 there were 450, a decline of 350 percent. Taking into account ordinations, deaths and departures, in 1965 there was a net gain of 725 priests. In 1998, there was a net loss of 810.

• **Priestless parishes**. About 1 percent of parishes, 549, were without a resident priest in 1965. In 2002 there were 2,928 priestless parishes, about 15 percent of U.S. parishes. By 2020, a quarter of all parishes, 4,656, will have no priest.

• **Seminarians**. Between 1965 and 2002, the number of seminarians dropped from 49,000 to 4,700—a 90 percent decrease. Without any students, seminaries across the country have been sold or shuttered. There were 596 seminaries in 1965, and only 200 in 2002.

• **Sisters.** 180,000 sisters were the backbone of the Catholic education and health systems in 1965. In 2002, there were 75,000 sisters, with an average age of 68. By 2020, the number of sisters will drop to 40,000—and of these, only 21,000 will be aged 70 or under. In 1965, 104,000 sisters were teaching, while in 2002 there were only 8,200 teachers.

• **Brothers**. The number of professed brothers decreased from about 12,000 in 1965 to 5,700 in 2002, with a further drop to 3,100 projected for 2020.

• **Religious Orders**. The religious orders will soon be virtually non-existent in the United States. For example, in 1965 there were 5,277 Jesuit priests and 3,559 seminarians;

---

11. Projections for the numbers of priests, priestless parishes, brothers and nuns in 2020 are provided by Dr. James R. Lothian, Distinguished Professor of Finance at Fordham University, and are based on historic figures plus current average ages and trends.

in 2000 there were 3,172 priests and 38 seminarians. There were 2,534 OFM Franciscan priests and 2,251 seminarians in 1965; in 2000 there were 1,492 priests and 60 seminarians. There were 2,434 Christian Brothers in 1965 and 912 seminarians; in 2000 there were 959 Brothers and 7 seminarians. There were 1,148 Redemptorist priests in 1965 and 1,128 seminarians; in 2000 there were 349 priests and 24 seminarians. Every major religious order in the United States mirrors these statistics.

• **High Schools**. Between 1965 and 2002 the number of diocesan high schools fell from 1,566 to 786. At the same time the number of students dropped from almost 700,000 to 386,000.

• **Parochial Grade Schools**. There were 10,503 parochial grade schools in 1965 and 6,623 in 2002. The number of students went from 4.5 million to 1.9 million.

• **Sacramental Life.** In 1965 there were 1.3 million infant baptisms; in 2002 there were 1 million. (In the same period the number of Catholics in the United States rose from 45 million to 65 million.) In 1965 there were 126,000 adult baptisms—converts—in 2002 there were 80,000. In 1965 there were 352,000 Catholic marriages, in 2002 there were 256,000. In 1965 there were 338 annulments, in 2002 there were 50,000.

• **Mass attendance**. A 1958 Gallup poll reported that 74 percent of Catholics went to Sunday Mass in 1958. A 1994 University of Notre Dame study found that the attendance rate was 26.6 percent. A more recent study by Fordham University professor James Lothian concluded that 65 percent of Catholics went to Sunday Mass in 1965, while the rate dropped to 25 percent in 2000.

The decline in Mass attendance highlights another significant fact; fewer and fewer people who call themselves Catholic actually follow Church rules or accept Church doctrine. For example, a 1999 poll by the *National Catholic Reporter* shows that 77 percent believe a person can be a good Catholic without going to Mass every Sunday, 65 percent believe good Catholics can divorce and remarry, and 53 percent believe Catholics can have abortions and remain in good standing. Only 10 percent of lay religion teachers accept Church teaching on artificial birth control, according to a 2000 University of Notre Dame poll. And a New York Times/CBS poll revealed that 70 percent of Catholics age 18-44 believe the Eucharist is merely a "symbolic reminder" of Jesus.

Given these alarming statistics and surveys, one wonders why the American bishops ignore the profound crisis that threatens the very existence of the Church in America. After all, there can be no Church without priests, no Church without a laity that has children and practices the Catholic Faith.

Yet at their annual conferences, the bishops gather to issue weighty statements about nuclear weapons and the economy. Then they return home to "consolidate" parishes and close down schools.

As Cardinal Ratzinger said, the post-Vatican II period "has definitely been unfavorable for the Catholic Church." This Index of Leading Catholic Indicators is an attempt to chronicle the continuing crisis, in the hope that a compilation of the grim statistics—in a clear, objective, easy to understand manner—will spur action before it is too late.

—Kenneth C. Jones, January 2003

Mr. Jones, I fear, is far too optimistic in hoping that the statistics in his book "will spur action before it is too late." In the post-conciliar Church today it appears that there is one, and just one, absolute, and this is—to repeat the words of Pope John Paul II—that the little seed planted by Pope John XXIII has become "a tree which has spread its majestic and mighty branches over the vineyard of the Lord," and that "It has given us many fruits in these 35 years of life, and it will give us many more in the years to come." I cannot imagine any bishop in the world, no matter how orthodox in his personal belief, no matter how generous to traditional Catholics in authorizing the celebration of the Traditional Latin Mass, who would have the courage to dissent from the insistence of Cardinal Basil Hume that there must be no turning back from the policies adopted to implement the Council.

As Mr. Jones has proved, we are witnessing not the renewal but the "accelerated decomposition of Catholicism."

This is a fact and it remains a fact no matter how often and how insistently those in authority in the Church claim that we are basking in the sunshine of a new Pentecost. One cannot help recollecting how, in the years following the Russian Revolution, when the enforced collectivization of the land had brought Russia to the edge of starvation, official bulletins assured the Russian people week after week, month after month, year after year, that never before in their history had they enjoyed so high a standard of living.

In *Liturgical Time Bombs* I have alleged no more than was alleged by Cardinal Ratzinger when he wrote: "I am convinced that the crisis in the Church that we are experiencing is to a large extent due to the disintegration of the liturgy . . ." (See p. 37.) In his address to the bishops of Chile on July 13, 1988, the Cardinal explained:

> The second Vatican Council has not been treated as a part of the entire living Tradition of the Church, but as an end of Tradition, a new start from zero. The truth is that this particular Council defined no dogma at all, and deliberately chose to remain on a modest level, as a merely pastoral council; and yet many treat it as though it had made itself into a sort of superdogma which takes away the importance of all the rest. This idea is made stronger by things that are now happening. That which previously was considered most holy—the form in which the liturgy was handed down—suddenly appears as the most forbidden of all things, the one thing that can safely be prohibited.

Every Catholic devoted to the Traditional Latin Mass must pray each day for our Holy Father, and pray that he will remove every restriction from the celebration of the rite of Mass which Cardinal Newman stated (in *Loss and Gain*) that he could attend forever and not be tired, and which Father Faber described as "the most beautiful thing this side of Heaven."

Appendix III

The Right of Any Priest
Of the Roman Rite to Offer Mass
According to the 1962 Missal

In a letter Protocol No. 500/90 of the Pontifical Commission *Ecclesia Dei,* signed by its first President, Augustin
Cardinal Mayer, sent to the National Conference of Catholic
Bishops (USA) on March 20, 1991, it was explained that: "A
special *'Commissio Cardinalitia ad hoc ipsum instituta'*
[Commission of Cardinals instituted for this specific pur-
pose] charged with reviewing the use made of the 1984
indult [*Quattuor abhinc annos*] met in December of 1986. At
that time the Cardinals unanimously agreed that the conditions laid down in *Quattuor abhinc annos* were too
restrictive and should be relaxed." This special Commission
of Cardinals laid down a series of norms regarding the use
of the Missal, the fourth of which states that when celebrating in Latin, every priest is free to choose between the
Missal of Paul VI (1970)[1] and that of John XXIII (1962), and
in either case the rubrics and calendar of the chosen Missal
must be used. (The 1962 Missal is, in every essential
respect, the Missal of 1570—the Traditional Latin Missal of
the Roman Rite, the "Tridentine" Missal issued by Pope St.
Pius V.)

Cardinal Alfons Stickler was a member of this Commission of nine Cardinals, and during a lecture given in the

---

1. The New Rite of Mass (*Novus Ordo Missae*) was promulgated by Pope
Paul VI on April 6, 1969 and came into effect on November 30, 1969, but
this was not yet a complete Missal; the calendar and all the Propers of the
1962 Missal were still in use. The complete Missal of Pope Paul VI was promulgated on March 26, 1970, but its introduction was postponed until
November 20, 1971. The Missal of Paul VI is referred to as the 1970 Missal.

New York area in May 1995 he stated that the nine Cardinals had confirmed unanimously that no bishop may prohibit a priest from using the Missal of 1962 when celebrating Mass in Latin. (See *The Latin Mass* magazine, Summer 1995, p. 14.) In the faculties granted to the *Ecclesia Dei* Commission on October 18, 1998, the Commission of Cardinals is cited directly. The *Ecclesia Dei* Commission is given ". . . the faculty of granting to all who seek it the use of the Roman Missal according to the 1962 edition, and according to the norms proposed in December, 1986 by the Commission of Cardinals constituted for this very purpose, the diocesan bishop having been informed." It is thus clear that any priest of the Roman Rite has the right to have recourse to the 1962 Traditional Latin Missal.

On May 24, 2003 there took place one of the most important events in the rise of the Roman Rite since its virtual but illicit prohibition in 1970. Dario Cardinal Castrillón Hoyos, Prefect of the Congregation for the Clergy, celebrated a Pontifical Mass, for a congregation of thousands, according to the Missal of St. Pius V, in the Basilica of St. Mary Major—where the tomb of St. Pius V is located, a point stressed by the Cardinal in his homily: "Today a providential coincidence enables us to render worship to God according to the Roman Missal of St. Pius V, whose mortal remains are interred in this Basilica."

The Cardinal assured the congregation that the Rite of St. Pius V—the Traditional Latin Mass—cannot be considered to be extinct (to have been abrogated): "*Non si può considerare che il rito detto di San Pio V sia estinto.*" He cited Article 4 of the Constitution on the Sacred Liturgy, which stated: "This most sacred Council declares that holy Church holds all lawfully acknowledged rites to be of equal authority and dignity: that she wishes to preserve them in the future and to foster them in every way . . ." To their great delight, he assured the vast congregation: "The ancient Roman Rite conserves in the Church its right of citizenship at the heart of the pluriformity of Catholic Rites, both Latin and Eastern (*L'antico rito romano conserva dunque nella*

Chiesa il suo diritto di cittadinanza in seno alla multiformità dei riti cattolici sia latini che orientali)."

These statements appear to be a clear admission, at the very highest level, of the conclusion of the 1986 Commission of Cardinals that when celebrating in Latin, every priest of the Roman Rite has the right to choose between the Missals of 1962 and 1970.

This is also the opinion of Cardinal Medina Estévez, who retired as Prefect of the Congregation for Divine Worship and the Sacraments in 2003. In an interview published in the Spring 2003 issue of *The Latin Mass Magazine* (page 9), the Cardinal stated:

> The Pope urges the bishops to be generous and open to those [traditionalist] Catholics who should not be marginalized or treated as "second class" members of the Catholic community. I personally believe that ample guarantees should be given to Catholic traditionalists whose only desire is to follow an approved and legitimate rite. At a time in history when "pluralism" enjoys a right of "citizenship," why not recognize the same right to those who wish to celebrate the liturgy the way it was done for over four centuries?

> I studied carefully the question of the abrogation of the rite of St. Pius V after Vatican Council II. . . . On the basis of my research, I cannot conclude that the rite of St. Pius V[2] was ever abrogated. Some think it was. Others take a different view. And so, as the Latin goes, *in dubiis, libertas* [where there is doubt, there is freedom].

----

2. It must be stressed that the Traditional Latin Mass is far more than four centuries old and that Pope St. Pius V did not promulgate a new rite of Mass (*novus ordo Missae*) in 1570. The essence of the reform of St. Pius V was, like that of Pope St. Gregory the Great (590-604), respect for tradition. In a letter to *The Tablet* published on July 24, 1971, Father David Knowles, who was Britain's most distinguished Catholic scholar until his death in 1974, pointed out: "The Missal of 1570 was indeed the result of instructions given at Trent, but it was, in fact, as regards the Ordinary, Canon, Proper of the time and much else, a replica of the Roman Missal of 1474, which in its turn repeated in all essentials the practice of the Roman Church of the

---

epoch of Innocent III [1198-1216], which itself derived from the usage of Gregory the Great and his successors in the seventh century." Moreover, there is proof beyond doubt that the core of our traditional Canon, from the *Quam oblationem* (the prayer before the Consecration), including the sacrificial prayer after the Consecration, was in existence by the end of the 4th century. See pp. 16, 39 of my booklet *A Short History of the Roman Mass*.

The classic history of Vatican II!! . . .

THE RHINE FLOWS INTO THE TIBER

A History of Vatican II

By Fr. Ralph Wiltgen, S.V.D.

No. 0092. 304 Pp. PB. Imprimatur. ISBN 0-89555-186-1

16.50

Price subject to change.

Unbiased, definitive, popularly written history of the Second Vatican Council (1962-1965). Tells it like it really happened. Filled with facts. Totally absorbing. Shows the way the "Rhine Fathers" took control of the Council. Crucial to understanding what is shaping the Church today. Pope John XXIII's pre-council commission had carefully prepared the official *schemata* for the Council's consideration, but these were voted out and replaced through the concerted action of a group of liberal European Bishops (from countries bordering the Rhine River) who had met previously at Vienna and formed their own preliminary documents. We are witnessing the results in the Church today!

Widely praised as highly objective and informative! Includes many Catholic press reviews from the U.S. and abroad.

U.S. & CAN. POST/HDLG: If total order=$1-$10, add $3.00; $10.01-$25, add $5.00; $25.01-$50, add $6.00; $50.01-$75, add $7.00; $75.01-$150.00, add $8.00; $150.01-up, add $10.00.

TAN BOOKS AND PUBLISHERS, INC.
P.O. Box 424, Rockford, Illinois 61105

Toll Free 1-800-437-5876
Tel 815-226-7777

Fax 815-226-7770
www.tanbooks.com

Also by Michael Davies!! . . .

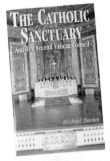

THE CATHOLIC SANCTUARY
And The Second Vatican Council

Documents that Vatican II and the post-Vatican II legislation did not mandate any changes in the Catholic sanctuary: e.g., moving tabernacles, removing altar rails, placing a chair in the middle of the sanctuary—nor even Mass facing the people! Quotes documents. A real bombshell! (5–1.50 ea.; 10–1.25 ea.; 25–1.00 ea.; 50–.80 ea.; 100–.60 ea.; 500–.50 ea.; 1000–.40 ea.). (ISBN-5476). *80,000 Sold!*

No. 1336. 44 Pp. PB.
ISBN 0-89555-547-6

2.50

A SHORT HISTORY OF THE ROMAN MASS

A short, authoritative, enthralling history (based on Fortescue) of the Roman Mass from the Last Supper to the "Tridentine Mass" as said today. Covers Low Mass, Sacramentaries, other Western Rites, etc. Highlights the reforms of Popes St. Gregory the Great (590-604) and St. Pius V (1566-1572). Says neither "reform" produced a "new" Missal, as was done in 1970. (5–1.50 ea.; 10–1.25 ea.; 25–1.00 ea.; 50–.80 ea.; 100–.60 ea.; 500–.50 ea.; 1000–.40 ea.). (ISBN-5468). *50,000 Sold!*

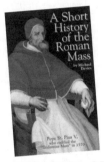

No. 1337. 53 Pp. PB.
ISBN 0-89555-546-8

2.50

No. 1283. 42 Pp. PB.
ISBN 0-89555-128-3

2.00

LITURGICAL SHIPWRECK
25 Years of the New Mass

Documents the disaster to faith and Mass attendance caused by the *Novus Ordo* Mass (1969). Though writing with respect, he says, "Facts cannot be loyal or disloyal, and the facts concerning the collapse of Mass attendance are, alas, only too true." Concludes we must return to the Traditional Mass. (5–1.25 ea.; 10–1.00 ea.; 25–.80 ea.; 50–.70 ea.; 100–.60 ea.; 500–.50 ea.; 1000–.40 ea.). *75,000 Sold!*

Prices subject to change.

*Cardinals and Theologians Cautioned
the Holy Father in 1969 . . .*

THE OTTAVIANI INTERVENTION

A Short Critical Study of the New Order of Mass

By Cardinals Ottaviani and Bacci, *et alia*

Issued in Rome 9/25/69, this "Short Critical Study" made several dire predictions of the bad results to be expected from the New Mass—which have come true. Yet none of the doctrinal objections raised by these Cardinals has yet been addressed by Rome. A most illuminating little book which includes the famous text, much other documentation, and commentary by Fr. Cekada. (5–4.00 ea.; 10–3.50 ea.; 25–3.25 ea.; 100–3.00 ea.).

No. 1190. 67 Pp. PB.
ISBN 0-89555-470-4

8.00

Startling, incontestable . . .

THE PROBLEMS WITH THE PRAYERS OF THE MODERN MASS

By Fr. Anthony A. Cekada

No. 1160. 44 Pp. PB.
ISBN 0-89555-447-X

5.00

The first and only study comparing the Orations or Prayers (Collect, Secret, Post-communion) in the Propers of the New Mass with those of the Traditional Mass. Concrete evidence that the Prayers of the New Mass have been systematically de-Catholicized of concepts including sin, Hell, God's anger, detachment from earthly things, Purgatory, conversion to the True Faith, merit, miracles, etc.! Startling and incontestable! (5–2.50 ea.; 10–2.25 ea.; 25–2.00 ea.).

Prices subject to change.

Ambiguous wording plus Liturgical "Experts" . . .

LITURGICAL TIME BOMBS IN VATICAN II

The Destruction of Catholic Faith through Changes in Catholic Worship

By Michael Davies

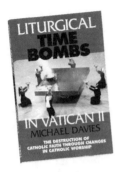

No. 1898. 96 Pp. PB.
ISBN 0-89555-773-8

12.00

Prices subject to change.

In this book Michael Davies shows how Fr. Annibale Bugnini—before his removal from office by Pope Paul VI under suspicion of being a Freemason—was able to "reform" the Catholic Mass into the constantly evolving liturgy from which the Church has been suffering since 1969. Quoting Bishops and Cardinals, as well as liberal "experts" and Protestant observers, the author points out the ambiguities or "time bombs" which were built into the Second Vatican Council's document on the liturgy by a few revolutionaries, in order to be exploited later—and which have been detonating ever since in liturgical abuses, both unauthorized and authorized. Michael Davies concludes with statistics showing the bitter fruits of the liturgical reforms in a massive loss of Catholic faith and practice in the Western World, urging a return to the Traditional Latin Mass, which has always borne great fruits in vocations, large Catholic families and saints. (5—7.00 ea.; 10—6.00 ea.; 25—5.00 ea.; 50—4.50 ea.; 100—4.00 ea.)

> *"I am convinced that the crisis in the Church that we are experiencing is to a large extent due to the disintegration of the liturgy."*
> —Cardinal Ratzinger, 1998 (see p. 37).

TAN BOOKS AND PUBLISHERS, INC.
P.O. Box 424 • Rockford, Illinois 61105

Toll Free 1-800-437-5876
Tel 815-226-7777

Fax 815-226-7770
www.tanbooks.com

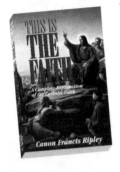

If you have enjoyed this book, consider making your next selection from among the following . . .

Prices subject to change.

Prices subject to change.

Prices subject to change.

Prices subject to change.

At your Bookdealer or direct from the Publisher.

Toll-Free 1-800-437-5876   *Fax 815-226-7770*
Tel. 815-226-7777   *www.tanbooks.com*

Prices subject to change.

Notes

Notes

Notes

Notes

Notes

Among the other works of Michael Davies
are the following:

BOOKS

Cranmer's Godly Order
Pope John's Council
Pope Paul's New Mass
The Order of Melchisedech—A Defence of the
  Catholic Priesthood
Partisans of Error (On Modernism)
Newman Against the Liberals (Sermons of
  Cardinal Newman)
A Fireside Chat with Malcolm Muggeridge
The Second Vatican Council and Religious Liberty
I Am With You Always—The Divine Constitution and
  Indefectibility of the Church
For Altar and Throne—The Rising in the Vendée
Medjugorje After Fifteen Years
St. John Fisher
Lead, Kindly Light—The Life of John Henry Newman

BOOKLETS

The Tridentine Mass
The Roman Rite Destroyed (On the ecumenical dimension
  of the New Mass)
The New Mass
A Privilege of the Ordained (On Communion in the Hand)
Communion Under Both Kinds—An Ecumenical Surrender
The Goldfish Bowl (On the disintegration of Catholicism
  since Vatican II)
St. Athanasius
The Legal Status of the Tridentine Mass
Mass Facing the People
The Liturgical Revolution
The Eternal Sacrifice
The Reign of Christ the King
Liturgical Shipwreck—25 Years of the New Mass
The Catholic Sanctuary and the Second Vatican Council
A Short History of the Roman Mass

About the Author

MICHAEL DAVIES, born in 1936, is of Welsh descent. He was brought up in Somerset, England and served as a regular soldier in the Somerset Light Infantry during the Malayan emergency, the Suez Crisis and the EOKA campaign in Cyprus. He became a Catholic in 1956 and taught in Catholic schools for thirty years until retiring in 1992 to take up writing full time. He has contributed articles to Catholic journals throughout the English-speaking world and is the author of seventeen full-length books and several dozen pamphlets relating to the Catholic Faith—the liturgy, in particular. His book on the English Reformation, *Cranmer's Godly Order*, and his history of the Second Vatican Council, *Pope John's Council*, have both been reprinted for the sixth time. His recent biographies of St. John Fisher and Cardinal Newman have been widely praised throughout the world. His book entitled *The Wisdom of Adrian Fortescue* includes a biography of Fr. Fortescue, whom Mr. Davies admires as the greatest liturgist of the English-speaking world, as well as a comprehensive selection of his writings on the Mass. Michael Davies has lectured on the liturgy and Church history throughout the world, including every major city in Australia. He has a special interest in the Western Rising in England of 1549 in defense of the Latin Mass, of which the final battle was fought in Somerset. He is President of the International *Una Voce* Federation, which is dedicated to preserving the traditional Latin Liturgy and has associations in thirty countries. This involves him in regular visits to Rome for discussions with members of the Curia, including a number of very prominent Cardinals. On October 24, 1998, Cardinal Ratzinger spoke to an audience of almost 3,000 traditional Catholics; representatives of French, German and English-speaking traditionalists shared the platform with the Cardinal, and Michael Davies spoke on behalf of the last. His work for *Una Voce* has taken him as far afield as the Philippines, India and Nigeria. The Federation spreads into more countries each year, and the most obvious feature of the new national associations is the very high proportion of members under thirty years of age.

When not traveling to give lectures or participate in *Una Voce* activities, Michael Davies resides with his wife near London.